D0924884

NOT YOUR JOB

Discover the surprising way to save time,

avoid burnout, and do what you love forever

Pierce Brantley

Copyright 2022 Invictas Publishing House

300 E. Davis #130 Mckinney Texas 75069

All Right Reserved.

ISBN 979-8-9870672-1-5

ACKNOWLEDGMENTS

Preston, this book would not exist without you. Thank you for your hours of research, editing, and for breaking my bad ideas. I am so grateful for your help and insight—and the occasional cigar as well. To Kristie, thank you for letting me mull over my vast trove of detailed and fascinating subject matter expertise in managerial theory with you. You never broke a smile and I love you for it. Mike, you're a genius. Thank you for your advice and helpful critique. To the Almighty—I still hear Your whisper, and it still proves true.

TABLE OF CONTENTS

GET THE COURSE

THIS BOOK TELLS YOU EVERYTHING I wish someone had told me about how to delegate. Within the following pages, you will find tons of stories, strategies, and ironclad management techniques—all of which have been battle-tested in the modern small business. Experience has taught me that growth-minded entrepreneurs often want more than just a book when they are building their businesses. With that insight in mind, I have created two additional resources for the person who is seriously committed to stepping away from the work that keeps their business in maintenance mode.

MASTER COURSE OFFER

The first resource is for the entrepreneur who wants to go a step further in their reading and truly master a discipline—someone who also likes a more immersive type of learning experience. For this entrepreneur, I put together a complete master course on the topic of entrepreneurial management. The course includes a more in-depth coverage of the strategies and techniques than this book format can contain. It provides hours of additional content to help you accelerate your mastery of the entrepreneurial management mindset and get insider learning from my personal case studies. The case studies include tons of new insights that come from my work with F500s and small businesses alike.

I designed the course to allow you to learn at your own pace. If you want, you can simply play the videos in the background and level up your business skills on autopilot. And as a bonus, I walk you through the templates in the swipe file and include some special training from industry veterans. If this is something you're interested in, you can access a deep discount of 50 percent with your purchase of this book. Use the discount code LEVELUP at https://piercebrantley.co/master-course to get started instantly.

FREE SWIPE FILE

The second resource is my swipe file of management templates. All the digital templates in this big pack are scattered throughout the book. For simplicity, I put them all in one place for you to easily access. The swipe file is free with this book and is available for you to download at https://piercebrantley.co/swipefile. You will find the templates save you hours of time in planning and training.

INTRODUCTION

WHAT KEEPS YOU FROM YOUR FULL POTENTIAL as an entrepreneur? Is it your work ethic? I doubt it. Is it your talent? Not likely. The single thing that will keep you from reaching your potential is limits to your own time. As your business grows, your time as an entrepreneur is slowly taxed. At first, it is a small tax—an hour or so on the weekends or staying late at the office once a month. You might notice the slight inconvenience, but you reckon the trade-off is worth it. You *are* a business owner, after all—this is the way it goes. But if your time tax is left unchecked, it will continue to grow as you take on new responsibilities in your business. Make no mistake: your business will continue to tax your time until nothing is left to give the growth of your company—let alone yourself.

This entrepreneurial time tax creates a reversal effect—even as your business becomes more successful, you have less and less time available to enjoy the fruit of your labor. If you do not address the time tax, it will increase until you overdraw your clock and deplete your talent . . . but that is not the worst of it. Eventually, you will have none of the freedoms entrepreneurship is meant to bestow—more time with your family or loved ones, more access to the things you enjoy, and more freedom to do the things that give you energy.

You see, most entrepreneurs start a business because they are intuitive and possess more than just a few special skills. They can see problems and solve them too—problems that the rest of the world may sense but still find invisible. The entrepreneur's friends and family call this talent. This talent is the typical spark that inspires them to start a business in the first place.

So the entrepreneur, encouraged by their loved ones and betting on themselves, decides to start a business to solve a problem and maybe make some money too. The entrepreneur applies their talent, their talent works for them, and their hard work is rewarded with a growing business. They have a dream that feels alive, and their hard work feels worth the effort.

But success soon comes with its own set of challenges. All successful entrepreneurs will soon see their dream grow beyond their own capacity. What they once saw as an overflow of talent stretches them beyond their means, and sadly, the dream holds them hostage to their work. Seemingly overnight, something horrible happens— the work keeps the entrepreneur from the dream because it demands both their time and an ever-expanding set of skills. This demand sends the entrepreneur spiraling into burnout—and this spiral is why so many businesses die.

In the US alone, entrepreneurial burnout is linked to over $300 billion in losses (Mol, Pollack, Ho, What Makes Entrepreneurs Burn Out, *Harvard Business Review*, 2018). The result is that many a good business will smolder away from a slow but ever-increasing stretch of the entrepreneur's skill and ability. The sad reality is that the business owner burns out because they have nothing left to give to their company—their talent and intuition hitting a wall as their effort increases well beyond what any average person can endure.

But there is good news. The solution to burnout is not more talent, hard work, or market savvy. The solution to burnout is to master a new form of delegation—one that leverages the time and talent of other people to increase your profits, time, and mental health. It is the single most critical skill a talented entrepreneur needs to grow beyond themselves. Without the power of delegation, you will be stuck in solopreneurship or a business that is doomed to an endless cycle of expansion and contraction—a cycle that ends in a blackhole implosion of business failure.

But delegation also presents its own set of problems. Most entrepreneurs are not born with management skills, nor do they have the time to go get an MBA. After all, they are building a business, and managing people can be counterintuitive to how talented folks work. While talent is all about leveraging skill, delegation is all about leveraging time.

For sure, some entrepreneurs are self-aware. They know their innate drive and talent are very different from the measured and mechanical work of managing people. However, since the act of delegation feels so foreign and the accompanying feelings feel so anxiety-inducing, most entrepreneurs continue to do most, if not all, the work themselves. This decision burns a little more wick on the company candle and slows the growth of their business. The compounding effects of extra work then rob the entrepreneur of the freedom the dream once promised. The dream demands time away from family; it limits the financial possibilities they might achieve and throttles the growth of their business.

Herein lies part of the problem. You simply cannot out-talent the time it takes to run a business. Eventually, no talent or business acumen makes up for the need to employ the time and skill of other people. This is why you must delegate if you hope to grow your business.

Delegation is the key to achieving more, earning more, and recovering more time. With the power of delegation, you get more leverage, more time, and more success—with less effort. But delegation is only effective when used alongside a special set of principles—principles that we were never taught and most of us were born without.

The good news is that delegation can be mastered. Delegation is an elusive skill, but once you master it, you can leverage other people's time, compound the influence of your talent, and get more accomplished than you could ever imagine. Best of all, with this rare but special set of managerial techniques in hand, delegation itself becomes intuitive—much like the talent you so naturally possess already. In fact, when good delegation skills become a muscle you exercise, you will find that you can lift heavier problems with greater ease through the effort of other talented people.

Let's get started. The sooner you learn to delegate, the sooner you will increase your profits, recover your time, and live the dream you pursued at the onset of your entrepreneurial journey.

HOW TO READ THIS BOOK

ENTREPRENEURS ARE BUSY PEOPLE. With that in mind, I have consolidated the main topics of the book here. Of course, I recommend you read the entire book through—page by page. You will get the most value out of it that way, and you will not miss any nuggets of skill the rest of your reading colleagues are sure to find.

However, in case you prefer to jump straight to a solution or managerial tactic, I have outlined the core ideas for you below. So, use this part of the book as a map—you can easily chart a course to the section that you feel best suits your journey into entrepreneurial management.

This book gives you a simple yet powerful framework to reclaim your time, train an employee, and scale your business by using a new approach to delegation. The approach is designed to work in steps. The first few steps identify where most business owners get stuck and how to calibrate your managerial mindset. The middle of the book focuses on the framework. I also give you tons of details and downloadable resources that enable you to step away from the work you will no longer do. The last third of the book is devoted to more advanced material—techniques and managerial concepts that allow you to supercharge your new skills. Here is the chapter breakdown:

THE ENTREPRENEUR'S DILEMMA

This chapter unpacks the exact problem every entrepreneur encounters on their journey to managerial freedom. It reveals, in detail, the reasons why so few businesses grow as they should and why employees leave their well-meaning bosses. Use this chapter to get clear of the hurdles that keep you from stepping away from unproductive work.

BUY A JOB OR BUILD A BUSINESS

This chapter unpacks the misconceptions of owning a business and the pitfalls that entrepreneurs fall into when they use dated forms of management. It reveals what you need to know before you can let other people work for you. Use this chapter to decide what kind of business you want to run.

THE MINDSET OF SUCCESSFUL MANAGERS

This chapter explains how to think like an entrepreneurial manager. When you think like an entrepreneurial manager, you avoid micromanagement and its hidden pitfalls. You will learn about Antivalues. Antivalues are sinister, subconscious drivers of business decisions that negatively influence the way we think about work in our business. When you overcome an Antivalue, you are free to focus on building your business and delegating work effectively. Use this chapter to activate your entrepreneurial mindset.

THE ELEVATOR EFFECT: A MODERN APPROACH TO DELEGATION

The Elevator Effect explains a key concept of managerial leverage found in the book. The effect explains the phenomena that occurs when you delegate in a specific order, and the specific benefits of abiding by that order. Use this chapter to avoid some common mistakes we busy business owners are bound to make when left unguided.

KNOW WHAT I KNOW—THE GROUND FLOOR

Know What I Know explains in detail the information someone, other than you, requires to be successful in their role as an employee. The chapter explains why knowledge comes before tasks, and exactly what an employee requires if they are to be successful in their role—without your oversight. Use this chapter to decide what and how you communicate with your employees.

DO WHAT I DO—THE SECOND FLOOR

Do What I Do introduces you to the method that allows you to model work and/or train an employee. It also unpacks a concept called The Triad. The Triad reveals the three critical things that make delegation possible: tasks, technique, and time . . . subjects the next three chapters will cover. Use this chapter to get familiar with the fundamentals of new-school delegation.

HOW TO CREATE MANAGEABLE WORK

The chapter covers the first critical concept of The Triad—tasks. You will learn how to structure work into manageable chunks for the employee to do. It will also show you how to keep track of employee work—work which you cannot practically observe every hour of the day. Use this chapter to build manageable work for a new hire.

HOW TO TEACH AND TRAIN A NEW HIRE

The second critical concept of The Triad is covered in this chapter on technique. It will show you how to onboard and train an employee for the tasks they will do. It covers everything from shadowing—an apprenticeship-type approach—to on-the-job training and more. Use this chapter to discover the best methods for prioritizing training and building good processes within your business.

HOW TO MANAGE A PERSON'S TIME

This chapter on time completes the study of The Elevator Effect's second floor, Do What I Do, and is the final piece of The Triad. In this chapter, you will learn about a special facet of time management that benefits your ability to delegate. It also includes the exact steps you need to measure the effectiveness of work done in your business. Use this chapter to become a better manager of employee time.

TELL WHAT YOU KNOW—THE THIRD FLOOR

The third floor covers everything you need to know about reporting—which is how and when an employee will communicate the work they have done, not to mention the challenges they may discover. Use this chapter to learn exactly when and how to set up a meaningful reporting structure.

SHOW WHAT YOU DO—THE FOURTH FLOOR

The last chapter on The Elevator Effect teaches you how to promote an employee into a managerial position of their own. Specifically, the chapter will help you weigh the pros and cons of promotion. It sets these decisions in the context of scaling your business and achieving your entrepreneurial goals.

HOW TO PRIORITIZE WHAT YOU DELEGATE NEXT

This chapter shows you how to prioritize what you do (or do not) decide to delegate. This chapter is tactical. To this end, it will help you choose precisely what work should be delegated now versus later. Use the chapter to get a clear idea of the state of your business and the work you will soon give to other people.

TWO POWERFUL DELEGATION STRATEGIES AND HOW TO USE THEM

There are two types of delegation: principle-driven delegation and process-driven delegation. Both types of delegation are useful to the entrepreneur, but they each look very different in the wild. Use this chapter to create a culture of work that easily moves away from you, the business owner.

HOW TO MANAGE FOR LONG-TERM SUCCESS

Our final chapter explains how you can get the most out of your delegation processes and keep your business working smoothly for the long haul. As an added benefit, you will also get some simple tools to inspire employees and build a culture that invites good talent. Use this chapter to create a proactive and committed team.

CHAPTER 1

THE ENTREPRENEUR'S DILEMMA

"PUSH THE WORK DOWN!" said the business owner. Their advice seemed to bounce right off their top brass, so they continued to polish. "Stop doing everything yourself. I am tired of hearing you do not have enough time. I am tired of hearing you have too much work. You have plenty of time and plenty of people at your disposal. Just get the work done."

The owner's words were not exactly Toastmasters material, but they had a point. Their elite, entrepreneurial management team was managing work—not people. In fact, what they were really managing was an ever-growing list of tasks. Sure, these folks got a lot done, and it gave them much to talk about each day. But in the end, they had very little value to show for all their effort because they did everything themselves. Since they did everything themselves, the quality and the output of their work steadily decreased.

You might think this business was performing badly, because of all the busy work, but in fact, it was growing steadily. The company was growing well, as were the high-profile roles of the managers to whom the executive was speaking. But all this growth was manipulating the time of the management team. The explosive growth rate made each new task and business need feel like the most urgent thing in the company—and this urgency eroded their focus as business leaders. In the minds of these hard workers, they were simply being responsible for the tasks at hand.

THE RELUCTANT MANAGER

Alright, before we go any further, I have a confession to make—I do not love managing people either. I barely enjoy people, but that is a personal problem. As a kid, I once hugged my computer, and I am still living it down. I do, however, enjoy building businesses, winning clients, and getting behind a really good vision. Those things get me excited. A business triumph might as well be Christmas morning sans the wrapping paper. If I could somehow unwrap all my business wins with kiddish glee, I probably would, but managing people is not a gift; it is a skill hard won.

Many entrepreneurs, like me and the ones I mentioned, struggle with management. We struggle because we are already so gifted in so many other areas. Take, for example, yourself. As an entrepreneur, you can credit a lot of your success to your ability to think and build in ways others cannot—or simply do not have the courage to do.

You may not say it out loud, but it is true. Your courage is the reason you have built your business to whatever stage it is at now. But courage takes energy.

When your business is young, you can single-handedly provide all the energy it needs. But as your business grows, that will quickly change. Once your business has grown a bit from the time, energy, and talent you have invested, it will begin to require more energy than you can give alone.

Entrepreneurs who hold out and continue to be their businesses' only source of energy struggle. The risk is inherent for every business owner, you included. If you continue to only invest your time, your energy, and your talent, you will soon see your business rise to success in one area only to then sink in another. This volatility will occur over and over again until you have no more energy left to give. The sad reality is that many entrepreneurs stay suspended in this volatility, believing it to be a normal phase of business growth. Inevitably, they are forced to close the doors of their business if they stay here too long.

Oddly enough, this revelation makes for an unwilling management candidate. No one likes to be forced to change the way they work out of necessity. Nonetheless, if you have discovered this energy problem for yourself, or feel you may be headed in this direction, you have a bold choice to make. You can either continue the path you are on now and ride the flux forever, or you choose to focus your energy and leave your unique mark on the world.

BUILD UP OR BURN OUT

Christmas week had just begun, but I was not in the holiday spirit. On the outside, things looked great. I had more clients than ever and I had just struck up a new relationship with a notable agency in the Dallas area that was good for my business—but inside, I was a mess. On average, I only got a few of hours of sleep each night and had not taken a day off in recent memory.

It was confusing. I thought I had what I wanted—more business than I could handle, high profits, and some strategic relationships to boot. But I was exhausted. To make matters worse, my newest project required that I work over the holiday break and New Year's as well, because a key handoff needed to happen before the end of January.

I was assured that the client's teams would be working hard as well, so I decided the new partnership was worth it and worked through the entire holiday season. The client, however, did not. We did not speak again until late January, long after the communicated deadline.

I remember sitting alone in my car, completely lethargic, feeling that I had somehow trapped myself with my own success. Was this how all business owners felt? I knew *Shark Tank* host Lori Greiner's quote "Entrepreneurs are willing to work 80 hours a week to avoid working 40 hours a week," and had always taken that idea as a badge of honor. But all the business I had won had worked me to the point of defeat. Yes, as far as entrepreneurs go, I was courageous. I could hang with the best of them. But somehow all that gusto was hurting both me and my business. From that moment on, I knew I had to find a new way to work. I had to find a way to do less and accomplish more.

At first, all you need is your courage to get your business off the ground, but eventually, things get unwieldy. You start to work a little later than you previously did. You start to learn a new skill in order to quickly complete a project or close a sale. Before you know it, you are the CEO, the CMO, the CTO, and the intern—and the worst part is the internship is still unpaid!

PLATE SPINNING FOR THE WIN

The simple solution for many business owners is to double down and work harder than they did before. In the past, this approach worked. Entrepreneurs manage the things they can control. The things they can control are their talent and their time. For this reason, most entrepreneurs resort to plate spinning. Plate spinning is the result of doing too many jobs in the business. It is what happens when we do what we know instead of knowing what we do. The result is that we trust our present skillset over future opportunity.

I have met some impressive corporate plate spinners in my day—I have even been one of them. These busy leaders can multitask multiple projects and work incredibly hard. But sadly, no amount of talent or work ethic can keep things spinning forever.

One person I knew would stay at the office until 11 p.m. on many nights and come in on weekends to keep their plates spinning. Most of the time they were doing the work of a direct contributor. They would do things like create a new flyer or write a blog.

Another business owner I knew played executive and senior engineer—never seeing their family.
Another consultant I heard of actually had three (yes three) full-time commitments and somehow managed to keep everything together—at least at face value.

All of these entrepreneurs had impressive work ethics. But that commitment to the grind blocked them from building a real business—free of burnout. Instead, their work lacked focus, so their business did as well.

As impressive as plate spinning is to behold, if you are the person balancing all of this work, you will inevitably face burnout too. I do not have to tell you that burnout starts like slow kindling. Burnout is never an overnight bonfire, but once burnout begins, the plates start to fall one by one.

At first, just a small plate falls—maybe a missed meeting or late report. But eventually, what once looked like an impressive feat of multitasking skill just looks like a broken mess. This managerial mess, caused by burnout and doing too many jobs, will only take more of your time to clean up. For many entrepreneurs, it creates a subtle feeling that their business is gradually slipping into a lack of focus.

PROTECT YOUR TIME

In order to keep your business focused, you need to protect your time. From here on out, you will reclaim your time through a new form of delegation. This new but very different form of delegation will help you decide what is most important for the future of your business.

Many entrepreneurs tell me that the old form of delegation feels as though it pulls them away from what is most important. This is because delegation normally comes from necessity—no one starts with delegation as an end itself. Most of us try to delegate because we find ourselves in a position where we have no other choice. Perhaps it is the reality that we must stop doing something and allow someone else to do it for us, that makes the topic of delegation so frustrating. Since delegation is typically required at a tipping point in your availability to the business, the need to offload work can feel like you are being forced into a corner where delegation itself is the only way of escape.

For this reason, taking on the role of management can feel like the business itself is twisting our arm—forcing us to do something we do not want to do. Many entrepreneurs even feel like the act of delegation imprisons them to the future failures of other people. At least, that is the fear. This sense of uncertain survival, not knowing for sure whether the outcomes of another person or team will be good, can keep you from handing over the work that will ultimately free you from your own future failure.

"Wait . . ." I know what you might be thinking, "I do not fail. I am Corporate Captain America! The reason I have had any success at all is because I do things the *right* way." If you have had this thought, I believe you. I bet you do have reams of historical proof that doing things yourself has worked out well. And you are right. You know how to do the task at hand.

The work, however, is the problem. The work you have done has led you to the river. Now it is time to cross the bridge. Blazing trails and building bridges are different jobs. You delegate work when the path forward is known. It is finally time to say, "That's not my job."

CHAPTER 2

BUY A JOB OR BUILD A BUSINESS

"AND PIERCE, THAT IS WHEN I REALIZED I was not really a business owner. I had simply bought myself a job." A small business owner said this to me shortly after I landed for a work trip. I still remember the comment jerking the jetlag out of me. Embedded in their words, however, was the secret to their new-found entrepreneurial success; a kind of success I had only dreamed of achieving.

You see, in my first business, I ran the show and performed in it too. I was the Taika Waititi of internet marketing, but I always saw myself as a bit of a mogul. The thought had never occurred to me that my old business was basically just a good ol' nine-to-five job with self-employment tax. The same was true for this entrepreneur until they discovered a new way to delegate.

A lot of entrepreneurs, including me, buy themselves jobs— meaning they get a skillset and then give it to the market in exchange for revenue. This works well for them. On the other hand, other business owners I know are able to scramble together a team, but the team never seems to function without them because they see the team as an extension of themselves. In both cases, the entrepreneur's existential problem remains the same: their role within the company will continue to grow when instead, it should actually become more focused. For the entrepreneur, a focused role produces a faster future. But I did not always see it this way.

I'M NOT JEALOUS . . . YOU'RE JEALOUS

Early in my business career, I remember talking to a friend, who owned a creative agency, about the number of clients they had. I was about twenty-two years old and working very long days. At the time, I was finding the upper limits of my time capacity to be around four clients. "How many clients do you have right now?" I asked.

"About twenty-seven," they responded.

I felt a little heat in my chest and swallowed slowly. *How could they possibly manage so many clients by themselves*, I wondered. If I am honest, I was a little jealous. I was working 12–14-hour days and never saw friends or family. *I guess I can work seven days a week and increase my hours*, I thought. *If that is what it takes to be at the top, I will do it.*

It never occurred to me to ask them how they were able to achieve a 5x multiple on my current performance levels. The reason, I discovered later, was in how they defined their role.

THE ENTREPRENEURIAL MANAGER

After talking with many small business owners, I am convinced that one of the key reasons we do not delegate is that we do not want to exchange our business calling for a managerial one. When I dig a little deeper, I find that these same entrepreneurs believe that their ever-expanding job title is a sign that something is going well. In truth, it is just the time tax increasing its claim.

I want to be clear about something: delegation is not a binary decision. You don't have to choose to either run your business or manage the people in your business. You are not taking off the entrepreneur hat and exchanging it for a managerial one. A hardline decision like that would be equally detrimental to your business. In contrast, when you learn how to delegate, you learn how to scale your entrepreneurial efforts. From now on, think of yourself as an *entrepreneurial manager*, which is different from that of *just* an entrepreneur or that of *just* a manager.

An entrepreneurial manager guides their organization toward a greater vision. An entrepreneurial manager also delegates work strategically. From now on, every new hire is a focused decision to bring new energy to your business and recover your time. Do not think of yourself as moving your role into people management. If that were the case, you would just be buying yourself a role in business maintenance. Neither are you just a solopreneur or a key member of a small team. You are now an entrepreneurial manager— a blend of visionary, guide, and mentor. This new role requires you to gain new skills and a new mindset.

Now here is the best part: you do not need to be a managerial giant like Peter Drucker to build a highly effective team. Nor do you need a big book on managerial theory to become a great entrepreneurial manager. You simply need to know the right steps—in the right order—to help people help you. Anything else and you are overbuilding your managerial skill set.

Start now and start lean. Many entrepreneurs never move beyond this managerial crossroad because they think they need MBA-level training to get good at delegation.

OLD MANAGEMENT STYLES IN A NEW BUSINESS

People tell me that delegation does not work for them. Perhaps they tried to delegate and got burned by a person doing the work, or maybe they burned out themselves by watching the details of work too closely. In either case, I agree with them. The old way of delegating does not work.

The reason goes back to the very word itself. The word delegate in the Latin origin literally means "down and away." This form of delegation is exactly what most of us have experienced in bad jobs ourselves. I cannot tell you how many times some old boss asked me to do something because they thought it was beneath them, or they simply wanted the task away from their desk. I bet you have similar stories too. The problem with this down-and-away approach to delegating is that it solves the immediate problem for the manager but creates a problem for the employee. As we know, these "employee problems" have a way of becoming management problems.

As far as the manager is concerned, the work is now being done by someone else. The work is under them, and therefore under their control. The employee, on the other hand, feels the weight and responsibility of their new assignments but may not know how to successfully complete the work to which they have been assigned.

What happens next is textbook: the employee does their best but does not do the work as the manager expects, which creates conflict between the employee and the manager. Everyone thought they were solving business challenges, but now that the employee screwed up, the challenges are interpersonal. Time gets wasted on solving personality differences instead of market opportunities. Everyone involved gets caught up in the way they are different and goes to their respective corners of the business until someone needs to check in on progress. And then the cycle starts over again. This old delegation cycle is exhausting, and it explains why so few people like the idea of other people doing work for them. Why would they?

However, modern delegation is not focused on down-and-away management. At best, the old style of delegation only maintains a business. The new approach to delegation is focused on innovation. Delegation is an up-and-over exercise that moves a business to higher levels of competitiveness and innovative thinking because of the way the work is designed from the outset. This new style of management creates a win-win situation wherein your business perpetually innovates, and your employees do their best, most creative work, without you watching their every move.

THE MASTER OF DELEGATION

What exactly is this new form of delegation? Simply put, delegation is leverage. Delegation is the ability to get a mutually beneficial return on other people's time and talent. It is the system by which you get more done using less of your time. When you do it right, everyone wins—both you and the person doing the work. When you learn this new form of delegation, you are doing more than just shrugging your work off on other people and hoping for a good outcome. The Master of Delegation can empower people and empty their calendar at the same time.

This new form of delegation gives you freedom because delegation focuses on what is most important now. Note the word now. Delegation does not focus on what was most important yesterday. The freedom you gain when you delegate effectively will manifest itself to you through the activation of a greater goal, growth plan, or milestone that you want (or need) to achieve—all of which are ahead of you, not behind. For this reason, delegation does not care about what has made you successful in the past. Delegation cares about what makes other people successful, which in turn, is a win for you, your time, and the future of your business.

Think for a moment about the tasks and jobs you do now. I bet the themes of work vary every single day, maybe even hour to hour.

There is a good chance the tasks you do now will not deliver the goals you want to achieve in the future. They are not designed to. The tasks you do now may be good tasks, important tasks, or even enjoyable tasks; but tasks and goals are as different as rowing a boat across a pond and crossing the Atlantic on a steamship. Rowing has its place. Rowing a boat takes skill and strength—perhaps even years of discipline to master—but knowing how to row a boat is not helpful if your ultimate goal is to chart a course across the ocean.

However, if you have never delegated before, the idea of asking other people to do work for you—work that, at first glance, is easier done yourself—may seem daunting, even unnecessary. "Why in the world would I ask someone else to do work for me that I know I could do better myself?" is a common response. This is a reasonable concern. If you have been at the center of the work for a long time, or you are the only person who knows how to do what you do, then letting go of work in order to manage work will feel irresponsible. Moreover, you may feel a very real sense of separation anxiety at the thought of asking someone else to do something that you are more familiar with doing. But the only way forward is to begin to let go of the work you are doing now.

You cannot go back. You should not go back. Your mindset as an entrepreneur has carried your company this far. But now that your company is showing you signs that it is ready to grow into its next natural phase, it is critical you complement this growth with a new perspective toward delegation.

CHANGE YOUR DEFINITION OF DELEGATION

Whenever you read the word *delegation* in this book, I want you to think about it in these new terms. I want you to imagine what it would look like if your business led by example in everything it does. I want you to imagine what it would look like if your business consistently designed new solutions to common challenges and old ways of doing things. Imagine as well what it might look like if your business was the first thing that people thought about when they had a need for what you offered. This is where this new definition of delegation will take you. Just look at the companies you respect most, and you will find an entrepreneur who evolved their idea of management with this new way of thinking.

You will not get to this new place in the mind of the consumer by managing people in the old way. The world simply moves too fast now. If you consider the great companies and business leaders of today, you will find a common thread—entrepreneurs who got out of the way but stayed in the driver's seat by paying close attention to the ebb-and-flow of their vision. These entrepreneurs are happy to say, "That's not my job." They know how to attract and equip the right people for the right kind of work. The first step in activating this new approach starts with a new kind of trust.

TRUST BEFORE TASKS

Where once you valued how well you understood a problem or how talented you were in a specific area of your business, now you will value your ability to trust someone else to work for you. For some entrepreneurs, this presents a new challenge.

Most people who really need to delegate come to the realization that they are strong in skill but weak in their willingness to trust in the skill of someone else. Herein lies the secret to succeeding in entrepreneurial management ... you need to get really good at trusting people, or you will not get anything done. Trust must be built up, just as you would build upon a skill set.

Where most entrepreneurial managers get stuck, however, is to resolve that a task simply cannot be done well without them. Like the captain of a boat, they continue to keep one hand on the oar of their business and the other on their map.

This feels safe.

There are two things they feel certain about—skill and vision—but this mindset gives a false sense of security. Business leaders who choose to do both visionary work and tactical work will inevitably make their boat swim in circles as their focus and time is split between two very different types of work. As John Knotter says in his book *Leader Change*, "Management makes a system work. It helps you do what you know how to do. Leadership builds systems or transforms old ones. It takes you into territory that is new and less well known, or even completely unknown to you."

The problem with the hardworking entrepreneur is not their work ethic, but rather, what they manage. Rather than manage a bunch of tasks, like so many frazzled business owners are known to do, smart entrepreneurs must begin the difficult task of managing trust. Trust is the bridge to better outcomes. Trust takes you into new territory. Trust precedes the path to delegated work.

TRUST COMES FIRST

Before you delegate work to a person you must trust them, but you should not just blindly trust them in hopes that they will carry the business for you. Running a business is not like a real-life version of the Tribal Council on Survivor. We call this passive trust, and you will find it does not go very far.

Passive trust is what most people think of when they think of managing people. I cannot tell you how many mastermind groups I have been in where passive trust pops up like it is some new phenomenon. It goes like this . . . for most people, passive trust is simply taking one of their spinning plates and giving it to someone else to balance. You tell them not to break the plate and to keep things spinning.

They say, "Okay, boss," break the plate, and give you some reason for why the handoff was never really a handoff.

You both get frustrated, clean up the mess, and at least one person gets voted off the island—or you fantasize about moving to some lonely island yourself and never working with people again.

Instead, you need to use something called active trust. Active trust is a type of entrepreneurial self-awareness. Active trust is different from passive trust in that it requires you to understand why you are letting go of certain work and why you are trusting someone else to do it in your stead. Active trust requires you to clarify why the work is leaving your plate to begin with. Passive trust only asks that someone sit in the seat and get the job done and erodes quickly when something goes wrong.

SLOWER THAN MOLASSES

Years ago, I hired an engineer to build an app for a large company and the ensuing fallout taught me the negative effects of passive trust. The person I hired had a great resume that included some relevant examples of work they had previously done. At face value, they seemed like a great fit for the project. Trusting they were the right person for the job, I quickly hired them, assigned them an overdue project, and left it in their talented hands to complete.

Their first week started off slow, but I was not concerned because the first week always starts off slow. However, the second and third weeks followed in an even slower suit. After not seeing any meaningful work accomplished for nearly a month, I told my director, and we jumped on a call with the individual (who worked remotely).

On the call, they promised us the project was going smoothly, but something in their tone seemed off—you know the feeling. Something about the Zoom-call-echo lacked ambition. We did not get any real answers from the engineer, so we finally pushed them to show us any in-progress work, even if it was not perfect.

As it turns out, they had been remodeling their home and had not done any meaningful work (aside from drywalling perhaps), but this did not faze them. They promised to work hard in the evenings— but at their own pace. We told them to just focus on remodeling the home while we found someone new to do the work. Yes, they were slow, but I was slower to learn the lesson.

In your business, active trust must be built systematically—you cannot measure it otherwise. If you do not build active trust, you will end up revoking trust when the work outcomes seem uncertain. As you know, your feelings of uncertainty may, or may not, be wrong. You combat these feelings and build active trust through a systematic approach to delegation, which you will learn in the following chapters.

DELEGATION AS A SUPERPOWER

Delegation's simplicity is its superpower. Anyone can learn to delegate effectively if they employ active trust. All it takes is a little bravery. The entrepreneur who steps out, forfeiting their right to control every detail of their business, will gain the power of delegation—unlocking a whole new world of innovative thinking, loyal customers, and devoted team members. These entrepreneurs are amazed to discover what they can do when they know for certain that work is getting done without their staying presence.

Best of all, with practice, delegation becomes more than just a helpful habit. Entrepreneurs who consistently practice delegation find that the skill eventually transcends the working hand and moves to the subconscious mind. Soon they delegate as an act of intuitive will. They delegate without even thinking about it—and innovative thinking happens without them ever prompting it.

Work of all kinds, from tedious to talent-intensive, flies off their plate with ease. Now they are no longer burdened with daily decisions that only serve to steal their time. In turn, the processes and culture produced by good delegation create a shift in their business that allows their teams to work together in ways previously never imagined. These happy entrepreneurs might, in a quiet moment, even enjoy the results they see from managing people, as long as they do not fall into Dante's third level of hell: micromanagement.

CHAPTER 3

THE MINDSET OF SUCCESSFUL ENTREPRENEURIAL MANAGERS

NO ONE THINKS OF THEMSELVES as *the M word* . . . a.k.a. the micromanager. Every M&!@manager you have ever met thinks of themselves as responsible. If you have ever been told you gravitate toward this way of thinking, I am here to affirm what you already know: you are misunderstood. You are on top of things. You would not care about the details otherwise.

Perhaps you have never thought of yourself as a micromanager. I get it. It is not exactly a Purple Heart—even though it does come with a badge. Either way, we need to talk about the overly controlling elephant in the room.

We need to talk about micromanagement because everyone does it in some way or another. You see, micromanagement is born out of a lack of trust and, to a degree, managerial skill. Micromanagement is not always a hyper-detailed personality. Some of the most giving, intentional people I know become massive micromanagers when they start to lose a sense of control. They do not set out to be micromanagers, but the work itself creates a Jekyll and Hyde complex when things get tense.

Every entrepreneur is at risk of becoming a micromanager. Micromanagement is the natural state of anyone who does not know the state of things in their care. You need to solve this before it becomes an issue. If you do not address it now, none of your sincere attempts to delegate will be successful. But micromanagement is easy to solve. You solve it by unlocking a special type of entrepreneurial self-awareness.

The manager who practices this type of self-awareness steers clear of micromanagement. Moreover, a healthy management style, which comes from entrepreneurial self-awareness, drives people to work harder, more effectively, and with less input from you. However, if you are really good at the work you are delegating, or even if you just think you are really good, it can be difficult to let go.

As entrepreneurial managers, we need to let the work go—we may even need to grieve the transition. Grief may seem like a strong word, but if you do not let the work die, you will resurrect it again, vicariously working through other people. And other people hate this—they will grieve joining your team. Before you know it, you will be Captain Jack Sparrow with a ship full of eternally undead employees. They will try to escape, but they cannot because you keep reminding them the real treasure is ahead, right after you review their work.

You see, the mind of the micromanager is the mind of someone who wants things to go right but makes them go wrong because they rigidly push someone else's work to completion. Much like pushing someone who is trying to ride a bike, the added force actually makes the person lose balance and momentum. Perhaps they gain a little speed at first, but they will soon crash from the forced guidance. It is this rigid attention to detail that makes a direct contributor's work less efficient. The way to evade this rigid approach to management is with mindfulness.

THE MINDFUL MANAGER

Entrepreneurial self-awareness starts with mindfulness. Mindfulness is a mental state achieved by focusing one's awareness on the present, while calmly acknowledging and accepting reality. Mindfulness is a critical skill of the entrepreneurial manager. If you do not live in the reality that your business and your role within it are transitioning, you will compete against the work being done in your business.

I say mindful because it is one thing to know you need to delegate—it is another completely to practice delegation when you feel the need to take up control. The implications here are great. If you do not practice managerial self-awareness, you are very likely to A) control all of their decisions B) redo the work yourself or C) take the job you gave them back and do it all yourself. This puts you right back in the old form of delegation. As President Eisenhower said: "You do not lead by hitting people over the head—that's assault, not leadership."

I do not know if Eisenhower ever played whack-a-mole, but he hit that issue on the head.

You cannot control work; you can only guide work.

This is why many would-be entrepreneurial managers are in an endless cycle of assigning work and then taking the work back again. Funnily enough, some people call this management. They assign a task, step away from the work, critique the work, then do it themselves. What they really manage is an endless cycle of their own stress.

Sometimes entrepreneurial managers do this passively. They realize something was done incorrectly, then they feel the urge to change something. At other times, they do this actively because they feel they made a bad decision in delegating the work. They attempt to fix it and step back in to exercise their expertise.

Avoid this cycle. If you feel the urge, realize that what you are feeling is separation anxiety and not business acumen.

ONE MANAGER TO RULE THEM ALL, AND IN THE DARKNESS BIND THEM

A business owner I knew had a micromanagement problem. The problem persisted to the point that they developed a piece of software to manage every iota of work in their business. On the platform, everyone had to log their exact work, minute by minute, every day. Employees would also check in on very small tasks like email and phone calls and meetings, and even rate low-level tasks for completion accuracy on a visual scale.

The employees did not get much done because they spent so much time managing their manager, constantly quantifying and proving that they were really doing the jobs for which they were hired. The business owner's intentions were good—they wanted work done at the highest level possible and wanted to measure the outcomes too—but they could have achieved this through delegatory skill and not an obsessive attention to detail.

When you personally do the work and are good at it, you are naturally concerned with the quality of the job being done. You value the standard by which you do the work. You value the knowledge and expertise and years of experience it takes to do a task well. But as an entrepreneurial manager, it is time to pass that baton. You need to look at what drives your need to control outcomes, whatever that reason may be. After all, you have bigger fish to fry.

YOU ARE DOING TOO MUCH, BUT THAT IS NOT THE PROBLEM.

Why should you choose to delegate work now? Perhaps more importantly, what will keep you from taking work back once you have given it away?

Some common reasons for delegating are the business has grown, you closed a client you cannot manage by yourself, your skills are starting to split at the seams, or perhaps your hair is looking a little more gray than salt-and-pepper. Most of these things are situational, meaning that something has come up that is forcing you to delegate—forcing you to let go of what you are doing. Perhaps you are losing sleep or mental health because you are doing too much, but this is not the real problem. Once you recover a little time or peace of mind, you will go right back to doing what you did before (or worse—create an app to watch everything).

The solution for all of this is simple. You need a higher reason for why you are choosing to let go now—and that reason is time.

TIME IS OF THE ESSENCE.

Time is the entrepreneurial manager's Maslovian need. You will not survive without time. Just like Rubie, my family's Corgi, does not like to be forced outside to take care of business, neither will you like to be forced to go out and do what you need to do. An abundance of time will actually have a reverse effect on you if you do not know the real purpose of your work. You will just go right back to where you were and your newly gained time will disappear.

Dr. Charles Richards, the acclaimed psychotherapist, provides us with time-honored insight about time and the recovery of it: "Do not be fooled by the calendar. There are only as many days in the year as you make use of. One [person] gets only a week's value out of a year while another [person] gets a full year's value out of a week." His timeless insight reminds us that time itself is not what we are really recovering.

REESTABLISH YOUR ROLE.

Delegation is about reestablishing why we work based on what is most valuable for us to do. By establishing what is most valuable for our time, we can freely and responsibly give work to others, so we get more leverage from our day. Time will recover itself if we focus our time on what is most valuable.

Good entrepreneurial managers know this principle. They manage from a set of values that govern and drive the success of their team and the business in which they serve. Your managerial values drive what you continue to do, and what you discontinue to do. Values always find higher aspirations. They elevate a person's work—most importantly, your own.

When we talk about values in the managerial context, we are talking about being aware of what we value most for the use of our time. Inexperienced managers use their time to watch work. Experienced managers, especially entrepreneurial ones, use time to multiply time. They maximize the talent and time of their employees so that everyone is emotionally invested in the vision and mission of the business. This investment, in turn, creates a culture of innovative thinkers.

Now values do eventually lead to a time commitment. Consider your values outside of work. If you value your health, you find time to work out. If you value your friends, you spend time with them. If you value chilling, you have a Netflix subscription. Your values force you to make decisions with your time.

So, if you are not a values-driven manager, then you will be a task-driven manager. This shift will happen without your realization because your subconscious is driven to complete objectives that you value personally. As a new entrepreneurial manager, if you are not mindful of what you value, you will be reactive, constantly jumping in to help other people meet their time-bound commitments. You will be blown about by the winds of the business, constantly changing course as the work tries to change priority.

GET FOCUSED ON WHAT YOU VALUE.

After years of operating within a managerial role, Gustav was demoted from his position as a manager. For some, it was probably a shock, but Gustav's colleagues saw it coming. You see, Gustav was a kind and gracious person. He listened to people, paid for their meals, and made sure his team was not lost in a sea of corporate bureaucracy. Where Gustav went wrong was in how he contributed to the business.

Gustav valued how he was seen in the company. He did not value the way the work was done by his team. He assumed that if he could fix the problem, the problem did not exist. He spent a lot of his time fixing problems. Because he liked credit for fixing problems, he allowed problems to fester—but it was not his job to fix things. He thought like a direct contributor and acted accordingly. He valued his image and his delivery when he should have valued his time.

For the entrepreneurial manager, tasks can become taskmasters— they will demand our time. Because of this, most people only realize they need to delegate once their tasks (i.e., the work) starts dictating how their time is spent. They cannot get away from what they are currently doing, and this takes time away from what they should be doing. At face value, this seems like an easy problem to solve—just start doing the more important things and stop doing the less important things. But any seasoned entrepreneur will tell you this does not work.

If you do not work from a values-based center, you will continue to work from a task-based center. You will delegate work, then take it back again because you do not know what drives and decides how your time should be prioritized. There will always be some priority that screams to you that it is more important than the rest of the present work.

Work is like a poltergeist. If you let it, work will move things around until you are haunted by its control—or you get sucked into a TV—that happens too. And if you do not know what motivates and drives your decision-making, you will find yourself with a conflict of priorities. This conflict is rooted in bad managerial values.

Until you get rid of these conflicts, known as Antivalues, you will get in the way of your employee's work.

THE WRONG MANAGERIAL VALUES

Micromanagement, and the conflict it produces, is rooted in something called the Antivalue. Antivalues are the antithesis of a value. Where values protect your time and give life to your business, Antivalues rob your business of growth and siphon your time. Worse still, they prevent the growth that comes from good management.

What are Antivalues? Antivalues are ideals we hold on to that are counterproductive to the goals and vision we want to achieve. Antivalues put our expertise over the success of the employee— keeping us in a cycle of operational mistrust. We all have some type of Antivalue we need to confront. And the sooner the better—you will never get good at delegation if you do not get rid of the Antivalues you possess.

The reason Antivalues are so sinister is because they speak to you in your own voice—justifying their own existence and preeminence over your ability to make good decisions. Even worse, Antivalues feel like real values. Antivalues tell you that you cannot survive without their guiding presence. In this way, they value past successes over the present momentum. They are also easily defensible because they are deeply personal. Antivalues are about you, and because they are so personal, they drive your behavior without you even realizing you are controlled by them.

You need to root them out. The faster you identify these potential bad values in your work, the faster you can begin to build new values to replace them, and the faster you can get work off your plate. When you take this crucial step, you will recover your time for the long term and avoid the pitfalls of micromanagement.

THE FEAR DRIVER
AND THE EGO DRIVER

The two main Antivalues every entrepreneur must face are the Fear Driver and the Ego Driver. I call them *drivers* because they drive you to make decisions that are neither rational nor in the best interest of you, the entrepreneurial manager. Every business owner deals with them differently, but both have the potential to keep you from reaching the higher aspirations of your time.

You will be relieved to know that even the most seasoned entrepreneurial managers struggle to let them go. What has helped successful managers overcome them is awareness. When you know the Antivalue you tend to adopt, you can avoid the tendencies that activate it.

Here is a quick summary of how they work: if you are *fear driven, you* believe that "x" task will fail if you do not do it yourself. Whereas if you are *ego driven,* you believe your significance is tied up in the work you do. If you are managing for the first time, you likely have some blend of both Antivalues affecting your decision-making, even if you do not realize their presence in your business.

One last thing before we unpack them. Neither of these Antivalues are true about you—but they will feel true until you figure out how to deal with them. And until you deal with them, they will deal fatal blows to your delegation efforts, replacing your well-positioned leverage with lies about unproductive work and perceived incompetence. Let's look at each Antivalue in a little more detail. See if you can identify yourself in them.

FEAR DRIVER

The fear-driven value tells you to believe "x" will fail if you do not personally do the work. The internal narrative of this value plays a script out in the mind of the aspirational manager and tells them that unless they are at the very center of execution, something will fail.

This fear will attach itself to anything—a small task or an aspect of some previous job you have done for a significant period of time. Depending on how strong this Antivalue feels, it may extend beyond a simple fear of failure. This Antivalue will conjure up entire fake narratives in your mind of angry customers, bad press, or worse, the loss of a business and your reputation—all in an effort to sustain a narrative that things fail when you personally do not do them.

BEING UNABLE TO LET GO

A senior software engineer dealt with the Fear Driver Antivalue. It surfaced when they were promoted into management and had to hire someone to replace them. As important as this new role was for their career, they could not let the work go. In the evenings, after their new developer went home, they found themselves jumping in to rewrite the person's code to suit their own style of development. This led to many nights where they would stay up late to fix subjective errors in their employee's work. Each morning that followed, I would hear this individual rant about how badly the previous day's code was written and how their expertise, as a senior in the company, was still required so the software platform would not crash.

In reality, it was their fear of the unknown, not their knowledge of how the work was done, that drove them to make changes to their hire's work after hours. The work done by their new delegate was fine. This person was simply afraid something would fail because they did not know how the work was done.

I do not have to tell you that, eventually, their new hire changed roles when they saw their work was deemed insignificant. This change was not just a loss for the new engineer but for the new manager as well.

The Fear Driver is relentless because it pits you against the immediate need, which you know you should delegate, and the ultimate failure it promises if you choose to get out of the way.

The Fear Driver will also make you take on ridiculous amounts of work because it tells you everything has to go through you in order to not fail. Nearly every manager I have met starts their journey with a Fear Driver. Left unchecked, it grows into a second Antivalue: The Ego Driver.

REPLACING THE FEAR DRIVER WITH GOODWILL

To fight the Fear Driver, we need to replace it with the value of goodwill. Goodwill trusts that people both want to do a good job and are capable of doing so. Of course, that does not mean they are as capable as you, but as an entrepreneurial manager, it will be up to you to make sure they succeed. We will tackle this in greater detail later with the principle *Know What I Know*. Until then, consider these affirmations to build up your trust:

- People are intrinsically motivated to do good work.
- Most people fail not because they are unskilled but because they do not know what is expected of them.

While it is true that we are no longer responsible for the work we used to do or know how to do, we *are* responsible for the success of others—and if we fail them, then they fail. The key is to empower them effectively. We do this by eliminating the Ego Driver from the way we think about our relationship to the work we used to do.

EGO DRIVER

The Ego Driver commands a belief that your significance is tied up in the quality of what you deliver. This Antivalue would never dream of giving up the work, no matter how frustrating or time-consuming it can be to accomplish behind closed doors, because there is something personally gratifying about getting the job done. *"You are the only one capable of doing this task!"* the voice of Ego Driver says. *"It would be irresponsible to delegate this work."* On the simplest level, you may also enjoy the work as well.

I experienced seeing the Ego Driver firsthand. Years ago, I was part of a team hired to help a service business build out its brand and online presence. The business had a good name, and they were growing steadily; however, when it came to their marketing, we kept hitting resistance when it came time to launch their new website. For weeks, we went back and forth but never got the site live.

Finally, after some probing in a meeting, the owner of the business exclaimed, *"I am the brand!"* This individual went on to describe how we could never separate the company's marketing efforts from them as a person.

This was a classic case of the Ego Driver. Even though this individual was not particularly egotistical, the thought of people managing something so familiar to them seemed impossible. In part, they were not wrong—every good brand starts in the mind of someone—but eventually every good brand must grow into something the consumer owns but marketing maintains. Sadly, the website was shuttered due to this individual's overzealous self-actualization.

The Ego Driver makes no separation between you and the work. You are the task. *"It cannot be separated,"* it tells you. But it *can* be separated . . . and likely, it should.

The Ego Driver is birthed from time spent in a certain role and type of work for a long time. Often the systems and way of doing things are so tailored to you that it is truly hard to cut the cord. The thought of separating from the old work almost sounds like more trouble than it is worth—at least that is what this Antivalue will tell you.

But if you truly aspire to leverage your managerial advantage, then you need to find identity in something other than your old delivery work. This is another reason why good values are so critical to someone who wants to grow their delegation skills. The sooner we separate our identity from the work being done, the better.

REPLACE THE EGO DRIVER WITH EMPOWERMENT

To eliminate the Ego Driver, we have to get really good at empowerment. Empowerment is the process of giving authority or power to someone to do something for you. But empowerment is not blind. Empowerment must be centered around finding the right person—the right person who can do the work with integrity. Integrity, in this context, is simply doing the tasks the way they should be done. The employee who does the work does not need to be you . . . they are not the business owner.

We will tackle this in more depth with the principle *Do What I Do*. Until then, reflect on these managerial truths:

- You are not what makes a task successful
- A task is successful because it meets certain criteria

- Find a person who values the criteria

The mindset of an entrepreneurial manager is the single most critical factor for determining whether all the following strategies of management you learn will fail or be successful. Without the right mindset, you will tear your own house down. Without a mindset that is values-driven, your business will teeter back and forth on your managerial fulcrum. You will throw your vision and employees off balance when your Antivalues drive you to make impulsive decisions regarding the way people work in your business.

When you master the right values, your managerial mindset will be fixed on a firm foundation—one that respects your time, your highest aspirations, and the hard work being done by others for you. You can begin to make managerial decisions confidently because you know why you are managing to begin with. You are now ready to reap the benefits of The Elevator Effect.

CHAPTER 4

THE ELEVATOR EFFECT: A MODERN APPROACH TO DELEGATION

MY FIRST ATTEMPT AT DELEGATION failed miserably. Things started out simply enough. I had a new client who needed an expedited project completed ahead of a big launch online. I understood the urgency and quickly sought out the best talent I could find to get us to the finish line ahead of schedule. In short order, I found a promising small team on the East Coast, in an office right next to the Rockefeller Center. The team checked all the right boxes—and I was confident I was free of all my Anitvalues—so I gave them a critical part of the project.

The team got to work immediately, and I saw their quick action as a sign that I had done my due diligence. Before I knew it, they were done with the project and handed over all the deliverables the client required. The only problem was that they went so fast I never had a chance to review the work in progress.

Unfortunately, the client reviewed the work before I did and was appalled at what they discovered. The work was filled with errors and lacked attention to detail. Of course, I shared their distress and quickly jumped in to fix things, but the client would not have it. Within a week, they filed a claim against the business, and I lost the account.

My failure was borderline impressive. I did not even know I could screw things up so badly. Looking back, my failure was predictable. I gave the work away, but I had not delegated anything.

Delegation is not a blind handoff. Delegation is entrusting someone to do a trained task with the expectation of achieving a certain outcome, without you doing any of the work directly. When you delegate something, you should get a value multiplier on someone else's time—meaning you get work done through the direction you give—and you also accomplish your own, owner-focused work as well. Each time you add another person to your team, this value should increase, multiplying the true value of an hour or day or week in your business. When you delegate effectively, everyone wins—the individual doing the work, the organization receiving the value, and ultimately you.

When you get into this managerial flow, you will experience a phenomenon called The Elevator Effect. The Elevator Effect is a new way of delegating, and it explains how the best entrepreneurial managers get more done using a simple process you can start today.

We call it The Elevator Effect because it takes your entire business to higher levels, almost on autopilot.

THE ELEVATOR EFFECT

In the past, delegation was a *down-and-away* form of management. Work was sent down to the basement, and the work was largely done in the dark until it was time to review. Modern delegation is like an elevator. It is an *up-and-together* form of people management. This form of delegation carries everyone to a known destination at a consistent, predictable pace.

The Elevator Effect has four floors—a.k.a. principles. Each time a person moves up to one of these floors, they gain a higher perspective and access to more responsibility. Each floor unlocks more potential for the business because, as people gain experience, so does the business. As an employee gains practical experience, you also recover a little more time. And just like an elevator, the work is visible to everyone, and you can watch people move toward their new destination.

You control which floor an employee gets access to and when. This keeps the reins of the business in your hands but gives the employee the agency to explore the floors they do have access to with complete freedom. In this way, you strike a balance between managerial guidance and employee empowerment. When you are ready to take someone up to the next level, you both reap the benefits. Let's take a minute and look at a summary of each one so we can get familiar with the concept.

THE GROUND FLOOR: KNOW WHAT I KNOW

The ground floor is all about communicating vision and what only you, the business owner, truly know. For now, it's where you spend most of your time and focus in the business. This is by design. You need to tell people what you know before you can tell them what to do. You see, at this point, most things about your business are in your head. On the ground floor, you reverse engineer what only you know and why it is important, so you can effectively communicate the work you need done. In this way, you paint a picture of where the employee can go and what they can do when they work for your business.

THE SECOND FLOOR: DO WHAT I DO

The second floor unpacks the fundamentals of delegation within an entrepreneurial context. Where the first floor was focused on the vision of the business and onboarding the employee, the second floor is where the real work gets done. This floor builds on the foundation of vision but expands into practical training and task management—things that are essential if want to step away from the work you used to do. The second floor requires you to not just show and tell, but to observe and demonstrate work as it is done.

THE THIRD FLOOR: TELL ME WHAT YOU KNOW

The third floor is the first move away from your expertise and toward the expertise of another person or system. Once you get to this floor, the individual doing the work will know more about the day in and day out than you do. This is where their role grows, and regular reporting is required. Here is where you use the reporting techniques you have learned to grow your business intelligence. This will keep you from taking up the old jobs you used to do.

THE FOURTH FLOOR: SHOW ME WHAT YOU DO

The fourth and final floor signals that your organization has grown, the individual doing the work fully owns the outcomes, and the process of delegation may need to start over again—only this time they will lead a team or initiative themselves and show you how this part of the business will be run. Once you make it to this floor, you will also have some decisions to make about how the person's role will change. You will discover how to grow their role without adding stress or extra bureaucracy to the process.

GUIDING THEM UP EACH FLOOR

We will spend the next few chapters unpacking each floor, along with its unique techniques, approach, and pitfalls in detail. As we go up each floor together, you will also gain greater perspective on how to build out and let go of the necessary jobs in your business—never to take them up again! When you guide people with the principles within The Elevator Effect, you not only help people help you, but you also unlock the power of organic innovation.

ORGANIC INNOVATION

When you leverage the power of The Elevator Effect, you turn old-school delegation on its head. Where once you might have been tempted to push work down, now you will send work up. When you send work up, you open up the opportunity for something called organic innovation.

Organic innovation is what we use to describe the little miracles that occur in businesses that foster managerial focus and employee freedom at the same time. When an employee is given this open environment, they produce solutions to all kinds of business problems that once fell squarely on your shoulders alone. When you employ the principles in The Elevator Effect, you let the business solve problems and create opportunities for you. If you ignore the principles of The Elevator Effect, you go back to pushing work down and making mistakes like I did with my Rockefeller team.

AN EXAMPLE OF ORGANIC INNOVATION

I saw organic innovation occur firsthand in a very small company, but the effects were huge. In the early 2000s, I saw this business go from about six employees to a strategic partnership and then finally, an acquisition, all in the span of about two years. The incredible rise to prominence included becoming a household name for their niche as well, but before all this success, the company was spinning its tires in an attempt to launch a new product.

For nearly a year, this company made promises to its customers that they were going to launch a new service that customers said they badly needed. The only problem was that the business's internal processes were not set up to deliver the service. The business owner thought they had the answer to the problem, so they anxiously hired outside help to try and accelerate their product launch—but nothing they did worked.

As the company went farther and farther past its projected launch date, the owner worked later and later, digging their heels into their plan to build out new infrastructure that would support their new offering. But they only fell farther behind. Eventually, they even ended up canceling the contracts of their outside experts because they did not like their approach to problem-solving.

THE SHIFT

Everything changed, however, when they finally decided to trust a new employee who recently joined the company. The employee knew about the problem but decided challenge the status quo. The business owner relented, and the employee got to work. Instead of focusing on the old owner-prescribed outcome, they studied the way the business delivered its existing product line.

After a little bit of research, they discovered that the old infrastructure could, in fact, deliver the new offering for at least the next six months. If the business would be willing to compromise, they proposed, and start the launch with their existing systems, it would buy the company time and help them keep their promise to customers. The only change would be some small tweaks to their existing website, which could be done in a matter of weeks.

The business listened to the employee and the launch was a success. Soon after, consumers were able to buy the new product while the new infrastructure was created. Timelines stopped slipping and the company soon made inroads into whole new markets. This organic innovation occurred because the employee was given the system, the focus, and the agency to grow upward.

You see, we often think of innovation as a big, heavily guarded approach to thinking outside the box. We think of companies like Apple, Tesla, or Airbnb as innovators. Innovation can happen organically, practically, and at all kinds of scale—if we delegate in the right way.

The business owner in our example discovered this the hard way, but you do not have to. Employees just need the ability and the system to take the focus of their work up, toward higher levels of achievement, instead of down into business maintenance mode.

THE BENEFITS

In the example of our infrastructure-tweaking employee, they were doing their original job, but in a normal company, they would have been asked to set everything aside and help the business owner execute their well-thought-out plan. The entrepreneur in charge had the courage to finally say, "That's not my job" and let this employee take a stab at the problem. What they gained in business success is nearly unheard of in the world of small business.

Obviously, not everything in business is about breakneck speed toward new products and innovative thinking. Nor should an employee discount your direction just because they have a problem with a particular approach. We have all seen businesses where the very ground beneath an entrepreneur's feet seems to be shifting on a daily basis. That's not great, but when opportunities do present themselves or problems do occur, as they will, it sure is nice to have the added benefit of organic innovation working for you as employees go about their daily work.

If you follow the approach outlined in the following chapters, you will see innovations like the one in our example occur in your own business—not to mention the constant benefit of reclaiming your precious time.

ONWARD AND UPWARD

The Elevator Effect is how great managers build high-performance teams and large organizations. It is also how CEOs and VPs get their time back and how super-entrepreneurs realize their visions faster than their competitors. The Elevator Effect also explains how you can have real peace of mind knowing that work is getting done the way you want it done.

Most importantly, when you employ The Elevator Effect, delegation becomes an exercise in trust—not just a list of tasks someone else must do for you. The implication is that you will accomplish work in a very different way than you have in the past. It will also change your expectations of how to manage and motivate people. Where you once valued how well you did the work, now you will value how well the work is done. You begin to derive this value by telling others what only you know.

PAY IT FORWARD IN 60 SECONDS

DO YOU REMEMBER WHAT IT FELT LIKE when you first decided to bet on yourself? For me, there were feelings of excitement but also a lot of unknowns. I think every entrepreneur has the same thought: *How exactly am I going to pull this off?*

I am on a mission to help entrepreneurs like us to bet on themselves and build their business. I love it when I see someone actually pull off their crazy dream and break free of the old mindsets and systems that used to hold them down. I bet you do too—and I would like to invite you to help me in that mission.

The only way I can accomplish this mission is by spreading the word, one entrepreneur at a time, but first they have to get past the book cover (and its reviews). If you have learned something new in this book, or were reminded of something you need to do, would you take a New York minute to leave the book an honest review? Your review will help other business owners like you:

- Spend more time with their family
- Build a scalable business
- Break free of time-taxing work
- Avoid burnout for good

It only takes 60 seconds (maybe less if you're not a big fan), but your help will go a long way.

If you use Kindle or another e-reader: scroll to the bottom or swipe up. It will prompt you to leave a review.

If you are on Audible: tap on the three dots in the top right of the app, select rate & review, and leave a quick note along with a star rating.

If you do not have this functionality: you can go to the book's page and leave a review directly.

When you leave a review, you help other business owners make decisions about how to prioritize their time. They might even level up their managerial skills—all thanks to you. Alright, this ain't QVC. Thank you for your consideration. Let's get back to it.

CHAPTER 5

KNOW WHAT I KNOW: THE FIRST FLOOR

"I HAVE BEEN IN THIS BUSINESS FOR OVER TEN YEARS," said the newly minted manager. "There is no way you will find someone with the same amount of experience as me," they continued. Their response was typical. For over a decade, they had spent time learning and growing a valuable skill set, which, in turn, had made them very successful. The time had come, however, to pass the torch. It was time to step out of their existing role as a tech expert and move into their new role of entrepreneurial management. But in order to make the switch, they had to get comfortable with someone else doing work for which they had more experience.

The new manager would have to be okay with mistakes, okay with different ways of doing things, okay with not knowing minute-by-minute details, and okay with what the person replacing them would do in their old role. Most importantly, they had to trust that someone else had the potential to be just as good as them. In this case, this was too much for the new manager to take, and sadly, they regressed to the familiarity of plate spinning. What they should have done was get out of the basement and up to the first floor: Know What I Know.

Know what I know. At face value, the phrase might sound snobbish. But you and I both know the statement is true. You are the expert. You know your business or industry or section of the world better than anyone else. Trusting someone else should not be done lightly. It would be irresponsible to hand off work without some assurances.

CHANGES

In order to grow into your new position as an entrepreneurial manager, you need to stop thinking tactically—seeing your success as the sum of how well you do something. You will also need to resist the temptation to simply offload work to the next person willing to take the job. Your role now is one of visionary and motivator. That means you know both how to find the right person and how to help them do the work correctly.

Now, there are a host of books on finding the right person to do the job. Who: The 'A' Method for Hiring by Geoff Smart and Randy Street is a great place to start if you want to get good at hiring great people. We are going to assume that you already have the right person, or at least a person, to whom you can start delegating work. Regardless, you are still the person from whom they must learn, so you need to get really good at knowing what you know.

Delegation can feel difficult to reverse engineer; compiling your years of experience and training, your hacks, your tips, and your expert knowledge into a standard system for a new hire does not feel easy. For this reason, many would-be entrepreneurial managers do not graduate from their founding role because the thought of getting what they know out on paper seems too tedious—even a waste of time. For these individuals, it feels easier to continue doing the work themselves, even though they know their role has grown past the work they presently do a long time ago. This is why floor number one starts with what you know—not what the hire knows (even though they are already capable).

The reason we start with the paradigm Know What I Know is because you need to trust a new hire knows how to do things the right way. Remember, trust is the foundation of good management. No technique will compensate for a lack of trust. If you do not know they know what you know, then you will take over when you do not feel comfortable with the way things are done. It is smart, and in your best interest, to teach a new hire what you know. You will both rest easy in your new roles when you do.

A FLOOR PLAN FOR GROUND ZERO

Think of this first floor as the foundation of onboarding. Where typical onboarding focuses on making someone feel welcome, we are, in contrast, focused on the new hire getting as close as possible to autonomy—working without your oversight.

To the extent that you do not equip, you will control. To the extent you control, you will cause headaches, workplace stress, and even the loss of your new recruit to another employer. So, trust and autonomy are where we start.

Your floor plan for the first floor is defined by four things. They are as follows:

History—Why you do things the way you do them

Vision—What the higher goal of the business is

Language—Why you use certain words and acronyms

Role—What is essential to the hire's job

We start with these four things because they give the new hire a reason to care about the work they do. If they care about their work, they will take ownership in their role. Better still, you will care less about the details of their day, and you will both get more done. These four things are a benefit to you as well. When you begin with these four things versus throwing the employee directly into the tasks at hand, you prevent yourself from jumping straight into the how of the job.

Here is what we mean. The temptation, with any new hire, is to offload the work quickly so you can recover your time and refocus on what is important to you. Because your time is valuable, it is easy to jump straight to the how of a job, and the how can feel like the most urgent part of a new hire's role—even though it is not. Take Rebekah for example.

REBEKAH'S MISTAKE

Rebekah was the founder of a startup in downtown Dallas and desperately needed help with the accounting processes in her business. She scrambled to find the right candidate and quickly brought on a person who she thought had the right skill set for the job. Relieved her financial headaches were over, she quickly threw all the responsibility of bookkeeping onto her new money manager and went back to doing the creative aspect of her business, which she greatly enjoyed.

Her business continued to thrive, but her accountant was crushed by the work. As the business grew, Rebekah piled on paperwork and frantically pushed her accountant to keep up. In short order, her accountant was no longer a fit for the role and was terminated.

Rebekah was frustrated her accountant was not able to keep up, but she never realized her accountant did not feel connected to her role—likely because they felt used by Rebekah. If Rebekah had spent a little time framing the importance of the role, with the backdrop of the company's history, and the need for the role itself, the accountant would have been more inclined to stay and see her role as critical to the growth of the company.

Yes, it may *feel* unimportant, but you need to resist the temptation to offload work until you have told your hire the history, vision, and language that makes their role meaningful. If you jump straight into tactical work, which is the second position, *Do What I Do*, you will miss a critical part of what makes a person successful at their job: culture and context.

CULTURE

"Why" will not win the game alone. This does not mean, however, that you should be quippy and inspirational for someone to enjoy their job. I knew a VP who always took one of their new hires through a workshop that had the person identify their personal "why" for doing their job. The executive played off Simon Sinek's book, Start with Why, and used the ideas to help individuals find personal motivation for doing their work.

At the start of the onboarding workshop, employees would give answers for why their work was important. They would enthusiastically start off with knee-jerk answers like "make sales for the company" and "be a team player." The senior manager would then gently guide them to answers like "provide for my daughter so she can have a better life." The workshop was inspirational and by all accounts, the employees enjoyed the shift in perspective, but the exercise lacked a connection to the culture of the business itself.

Eventually, new hires would still leave when their job became tough, taking their why with them.

CULTIVATING CULTURE

Cultivate culture to make delegation stick. Culture, in a business, is anything an individual or organization does habitually. New hires need to know why you do things the way you do them and say things the way you say them. They need to know these things to have greater context and connection to their role. If you skip this critical piece of onboarding, then the individual will eventually take their "why" with them—meaning they will provide for their family somewhere else or take their personal inspiration for working along with them when the job you give them gets too hard, or they do not understand your reasoning for important decisions.

For this reason, if someone ever stops working for your business, try not to jump to the conclusion that the person lacks vision or a sense of drive. There are endless options for employment, and a new hire deserves to know why they should commit their talents and time to your business. An A Player on one of my teams left for the simple reason that their *why* no longer felt connected to that of the business. That was a mistake on my part, not the talent or work ethic of my team member.

While it is true you may not be able to prevent employee churn outright, you can certainly keep people longer by connecting them to a greater cause—the deeper, practical importance of why they do what they do. Think of this step as risk aversion. Culture is not just ethereal; it is the day-in-day-out decisions that govern what is good about a particular role and the business at large. Ultimately, culture is fruition, grown from the history of your business.

In November of 1862, Henry Thoreau, the poet, philosopher, and mega-corporate-mogul, published an essay in *The Atlantic* called "Wild Apples." In his essay, he mused about the connection between the apple tree and humanity itself. "It is remarkable how closely the history of the apple tree is connected with that of man," he famously said. He was not just waxing about apple sauce and pie either. At the end of his essay, he lamented that future generations may not even know or enjoy apples, and that the apple itself would be forgotten over time. Ethereal though his words may be, his musings do help the business owner.

Your business history, and the fruit of it, is the outcome of what you have chosen to steward so far. Soon your role of stewardship will grow beyond you and will continue into the work life of other people. For this reason, you must connect the work someone does to the history of why it is done. If you do not, the talent you hire will eventually forget why they are investing themselves in your business at all. So, you make this connection in the mind of the employee on purpose. With this connection, this tie to stewardship, you build a solid foundation for your business's culture. Culture then actively supports the roles of those who serve your company.

You meaningfully anchor the hire to their work when you start with the history of the company and the importance of their role. A person who knows the history of the company is less likely to leave when their job is inevitably stressful. The reason is that they now play an active role in the story of the business. Not only this, but they will also be more willing to overcome obstacles on their own initiative, apart from you.

WHAT IS GOOD CULTURE?

Good work is good culture. A friend of mine had a long career with a major retailer. Eventually, the time came for him to move into a greater role at a new company in an even newer industry. What fascinated me, however, was how much he talked about the company, and not the role itself, when he first joined the new company.

Seemingly overnight, he became an expert in the industry and its competitive landscape. What made me smile most, though, was how clearly he understood the way in which his role would help people who needed the service the company provided. Incredibly, his passion for the role began before he'd even accepted an offer. This is because the history of the business anchored him to the day-in-day-out work.

His new work was with a startup, so you could argue that his role did not need all that context. After all, he never talks to customers or engages with the marketing team—but this would be short-sighted. When a person knows their work is connected to something larger than themselves, they will rise to the occasion. In fact, a study by Elizabeth Medina, research shows that job turnover in an organization with a high company culture is as low as 13.9 percent (Medina, Elizabeth, 2012 Job Satisfaction and Employee Turnover Intention: What does Organizational Culture Have To Do With It?)

HISTORY

When you tell a new hire about the history of your business, you must do so in two parts—you must communicate the business's reason for being and the role's reason for being.

BUSINESS HISTORY

The business's reason for being is directly connected to the problems in the market, why the company was founded, and how the company got to where it is today. This includes things like the competitive landscape, when the company was founded, and why you started and/or joined the company yourself. The goal here is to instill a sense of heritage in the employee.

ROLE HISTORY

The role's history should play off the business history. What opportunity did the company pursue or achieve that made the new role relevant? Tie the role to the future success of the company. The new hire is now making history and not just learning about it.

Whenever a colleague introduces me to a new hire, I always start the introduction by telling their team member about how long we searched for them and how much we need them. "We have looked for you everywhere!" I say, and continue to give them a quick summation of the amount of time spent searching for the right person, recounting all the candidates that did not make the cut. This never fails to get a big smile as the individual realizes they are critical to something bigger than themselves.

You might think that telling a new hire about the history of the business will feel like a waste of time, especially if their work is more tactical, or the role filled is an urgent one. But if you have "the right person on the bus," as Jim Collins famously describes in his book Good to Great, then you want to give them a sense of where they are going—this way, they stay around for the ride.

To be clear, you do not need to spend a lot of time mulling over all the historical artifacts either. This is not a museum exhibit (unless you operate one), so 15–20 minutes during their initial training or as a focused topic during lunch is fine. Just do not skip the step.

VISION

The second part of this floor is vision. If history is where you have been, then vision is where you are going. Vision elevates both the role and the business beyond the role and the business. Vision makes any work existential—bigger than you or them or anyone. Vision is also a translator. When you offload work to a new hire, they will internally question why they need to do certain tasks, though they may never voice this concern to you.

Note: if an employee does openly question something, assume they aren't questioning your authority but are simply trying to be efficient in their work. If you do not communicate the vision, they may have a harder time accepting why they need to do certain tasks to your standard. Vision translates the work they do, no matter how menial, into important work.

Again, this does not mean you need to be long-winded or have some huge presentation planned out. You are not creating a State of the Union address—just a quick primer into the importance of the company and the new hire's role therein.

A cyber security company I worked for articulated its vision in a powerful way. On my first day at the new office, I was depressed to see a big office full of empty cubicles (even though the company employed thousands of people). To make matters worse, I had to go through a strict screening process to even get inside the building. Before I could get to the real office, I had to step inside a small room, about 10 square feet in total, and ring an old doorbell next to a door with a small, shaded window. Cold, fluorescent lights beamed down on me while I waited for someone to look out the small window and verify I had access to the office. The whole process felt something like an interrogation center.

But my perspective quickly changed during a call with the CEO. During an all-hands meeting, the executive framed the team's work differently; he reminded us that we were at the bleeding edge of technology—we were saving the livelihood of real people and small businesses everywhere. We were Sparta in the movie 300. We were the Chicago Bulls in 1995. We were taking care of business—single-handedly taking down Russian hackers and bad actors in foreign governments.

Suddenly the work did not feel as cold and analytical as it did before. The overly cautious, TSA-like security was now adventurous. Of course we were careful who we let in! We managed over a billion devices on a daily basis, and we were preventing the next world war! The reason for the shift in thinking was the vision.

Vision is the greater goal of the business. Every business has one. You do not have to be a large non-profit organization or have a story-driven business, like Bumble or Toms Shoes, to inspire people.

SMALL BUSINESS, BIG VISION

A social media company I knew was making headway in a new niche of marketing where small businesses were known to struggle. To watch the employees work, you would think they were just browsing Facebook all day. Day after day, they'd write posts, schedule posts, and comment on posts. Watching the work would make one swear off all social media for good, but the company had the vision to help tell the stories of typically ignored B2B companies.

The marketers saw what they did as critical to the ongoing success of new founders and their young companies. They were telling the stories of people who couldn't articulate their stories for themselves.

This connection to the greater story of their clients gave them fresh drive in an otherwise dull work environment.

When you communicate your vision to your new hire, think of it as giving them a new North Star. You are giving them a role to play in something that is high-reaching. Vision, like history, has two parts: company vision and personal vision. Communicate both to your new employee.

COMPANY VISION

Your company vision is the greater good your business contributes to the world. Again, when you communicate the company vision, it does not have to be grandiose. You do not have to cure cancer or solve world hunger to have an important vision. To communicate your company vision, you simply need to anchor what the company does to why it does it and communicate how that transaction benefits real people—even if you never see those people.

PERSONAL VISION

Personal vision anchors a person to their own long-term goals. Give a new hire a vision for their future at the company by tying their talent to their investable time at work. Earlier I mentioned how I would greet my colleague's new team members and tell them how long we looked for them and how critical their role was to us.

Personal vision builds on this foundation. Where before it was important to articulate why their presence was critical to our success, now here you also want to communicate how they will be successful for the long term in the role. Simply put, you want the hire to have a sense that the work you give them will actually improve their livelihood and make their future aspirations achievable.

Tip: You can reinforce company and personal vision by combining them together in simple company events. The benefit is that people will enjoy doing their work and the event will create a culture that reinforces accountability to work—even when you are not present with your team!

One such example is with the marketing team of a company I supported. Every Thursday afternoon, all the marketers got together for an event called Champagne Campaign. At this special meeting, team members brought forward their most difficult marketing problems, along with weekly work, and solved them together over a few glasses of champagne. Everyone looked forward to the weekly event, but most importantly, the meeting created a sense of culture and an expectant future.

Sure, the team was talented and did not technically need the weekly event to do their jobs, but the leader who established the meeting knew that in order for the team to be continuously motivated, workers would need to feel connected to the work and encouraged regularly by their peers. Their idea worked and the work got done.

LANGUAGE

The third part of this floor is language. Language is the lung of vision. Language gives life and understanding to the way people work. Every company or career has insider language. We call it insider language because you either need to be part of the company or have done the job before to know what people mean by what they say. When someone does not know the language of the business, they will be timid and cautious about how they do their jobs until (if ever) they discover the acronyms, terms, and words that make your business unique.

The potential for timid employees is not a matter of aptitude. While it is nice to hire an employee who speaks up and asks questions assertively, it is not the best or even the quickest way to get someone ramped up on the knowledge necessary to navigate your company.

A director of an international nonprofit I knew nailed this principle. The director built out teams of volunteers all over the world. These passionate individuals helped tutor students in hard-to-reach areas and were very dedicated to their roles—often serving for years with many of them serving for free.

INTENTIONAL WORD CHOICE

From the outside, most people considered the tutors to be interns. They worked for free and also gained some free training. The director, however, never used the word *intern* and had a very decisive reason for doing so. The director used the word *apprentice*. To them, an intern was just a trainee who works without pay in order to gain a little work experience. An apprentice, on the other hand, was a person who learned a trade from a special organization, a trade that would benefit the person for the rest of their life.

Every time the director heard someone refer to the organization's volunteers as interns, they would quickly jump into the conversation and adjust the commentator's thinking.

Over time, he changed the perception of his volunteers from people just getting experience, to people who were building a better future and gaining life skills to do so.

Words have weight. Beyond just getting a new hire up to speed on insider language, that language also carries with it the culture of your company. The nonprofit director knew that the quicker you communicate the words that matter to your business, the quicker an employee will have the confidence and connection to their role.

INSIDER LANGUAGE

Now not all words are tied directly to the "why" of a business. Sometimes words just explain the "how" really effectively—and employees need them to get their point across in short order. A large Fortune company I consulted with kept a list of all the acronyms the company had created over the years. The list was searchable and made it possible to quickly identify what insider terms were being used in meetings. This made it much easier for new employees to adjust to conversations that were peppered with cryptic corporate speak.

If you haven't done so already, create a list of insider words and acronyms and share it with your employees during their first week on the job.

When you get intentional about communicating insider words, you set a good precedent for teamwork as well. A person I knew used to intentionally use heavy technical jargon to make it difficult for people to understand them. After a little bit of prying, it became clear they were intentionally creating insider language in an effort to keep the politics of the business in their favor.

Silly as it sounds, when you push for transparency in the words everyone uses, it makes for a healthier, more proactive team as well. You never know if the person you hire may eventually have direct reports of their own. For this reason, it is important to set an example of inclusive and transparent communication at the onset of their job.

Download The Free Template!

Get the **Insider Language** template along with other great tools included with this book at:

https://piercebrantley.co/NYJ-downloads

ROLE

The fourth and final part of *Know What I Know* is that of the employee's role. Of all the different parts on the first floor, the role is the most important. The role is most important for two reasons. If you do not have a clear understanding of what you are delegating, neither will the individual who is doing the job. Sooner or later, you will both get frustrated over mismatched expectations— expectations that are ultimately set by you. And without a clear definition of the role, you will end up dismissing the individual, or they will leave on their own.

The second reason defining the role is important is because of job quirks. Every job has quirks—little things that are different at your company and in your team, even though the title of the role is probably the same across the industry or even in the business next door. You know the quirks better than anyone else because you are the one delegating the job. It is in your best interest to communicate the quirks early on. When you communicate the quirks, you build two-way trust.

When you communicate the way the role differs in your company versus that of another, you will trust the individual knows the specific ins-and-outs of the role and the ways in which it is unique to your particular business. The individual to whom you are delegating will also trust you more as a manager because you are looking out for them and not assuming their experience or lack therein.

I saw this play out when I consulted for a healthcare company. The company had a deeply entrenched culture of legal process management, but for good reason—the company needed this process in place to protect its customers and employees. However, this had an odd impact on the way employees and contractors went about their work.

COPYRIGHTING OR COPYWRITING

One striking example was that of copywriting and the delivery of work to their colleagues. When it came to delivering work, employees were never allowed to use a flash drive or portable hard drive to transfer their work, even to back up their progress. In fact, it was a fireable offense to move work off a computer, and the process was strictly guarded.

In most technology-led companies, the idea of backing up work would be encouraged, and at the very least, an employee would not think they were doing anything wrong by doing so. But at this company, they had strict guidelines that forbade moving the work around. This problem was compounded by the definition of the term *copywriting* in the organization.

While helping a team at the company with a marketing initiative, I landed in a confusing conversation about finding the right person to write the content for their website. "We will need to find the right copywriter for your website," I said in the planning meeting.

"Copyrighting is done by lawyers," one of the team members replied. "We do not need our lawyer for this project." They continued.

"Sorry . . . copywriting *is* what I meant to say . . . the creative type of writer," I replied.

"There is no such thing as a copywriter," they quipped. "Do not make up words."

I went on to explain that a copywriter was in fact a title in the creative industry, but they did not believe me. "Okay, I said, what shall we call the individual? I want to make sure we are on the same page about the person doing the work."

"Creative website content writer," they decided matter-of-factly.

Done. The creative website content writer would be the one working the word processor—and they would be required to type their work at the office not taking any versions of their work home for editing. The conversation was taxing but not nearly as bad as it would have been if we had never gotten clarity on the role and its inherent restrictions.

Now you may not have complexities like the ones mentioned in this company, but there is a good chance that some of the tasks you are about to delegate are done in a very specific way. Some of those ways are for good reason. If it is important to the way the job is done, and the individual will benefit from the way you have done them in the past, tell them earlier on in their job so they do not get confused or frustrated.

JUNK DRAWER TITLES

You can avoid confusion and frustration with good titles too. I know you are thinking, *what do titles have to do with delegation?* I get it. Titles are a small detail and can feel like a distraction if the team is small, but for the employee, deciding on the *right* title can go a long way in keeping communication lines from being crossed down the line—if you build the role to fit. Titles are hard to nail down when the team is small because there is always so much work to be done. But the title helps define the value a team member will provide to the larger team. A good title also gives the team member something for which to aspire.

Because titles can be notoriously difficult to articulate, there is always a temptation to give a wide, but unfocused, title instead of being specific. I call these "junk drawer" titles because the tendency is to throw all the loose work inside them. As the old saying goes, this is exactly how some people get promoted to the level of their incompetence. The argument for this approach is that the business is in flux along with the role, so everyone should just keep things flexible. While flexibility may be a nice character trait, it is not a good title or job description.

I have seen employers try and attract top talent in job listings by using vague and hyperbolic titles. All this language really did, however, was demonstrate the manager hadn't thoroughly thought about the role. As an example, when a job title includes language like *expert, guru,* or *ninja,* then there is a good chance the person who created the role has a junk-drawer mentality for the person they want to hire—a.k.a. they know they need a person, they just don't know who. One of my favorite junk drawer titles was *creative genius product design wizard*. Yes. All in one breath. It would take some real black magic to attract a person for that role.

On the other end of the spectrum, I have seen employers give big titles to small roles. In one example, a director gave a college graduate the title of senior analyst. The work itself was similar to an associate-level role, but the title suggested seven-to-ten years of experience. The reasoning on the part of the director was that they wanted the person to *feel* important. But this created a problem within the organization because the new hire did not have the experience or the understanding to do the job. This in turn made it impossible to define realistic task-level work for the hire.

Keep your titles tight and aspirational to attract the right person. A good title is like a glove. It fits the working hand and defines the work ahead.

DEFINING THE ROLE

Define an employee's role in terms of successful outputs for the company and customer. I like to write a sentence or two that serves as a bucket for all the types of work the employee will do. Here are a few examples:

For a plumber: Your role as a senior plumber is to eliminate the stress and surprise that comes with leaky pipes, old homes, and poor construction. You think about the way a homeowner uses water, so they do not have to.

For a computer engineer: Your role as a front-end engineer is to create software that people enjoy. If you succeed at being productive in your work, they will feel productive on the platform you create. To that end, you use your expertise in technology to make the lives of our customers easier.

For a florist: Your role as a florist is to make people smile and feel cared for. You understand that each color, petal, and placement of a flower says something about what the customer feels for the person receiving the bouquet. You understand that a special occasion is one big colorful arrangement, of which flowers are a centerpiece.

Download The Free Template!

Get the **Role Definitions** template along with other great tools included with this book at:

https://piercebrantley.co/NYJ-downloads

Use these examples to prime the new roles in your own business. Doing so will give both of you a good starting point for the work ahead. When it comes to new roles, your mindset should be one of a teacher. The best teachers teach to their own benefit. They know if a student truly grasps what they have been taught, that everyone is better for it.

Master the four parts of the first floor, and you have a foundation for delegation that is built on trust. When your new team member understands how the business was started, how it contributes to the world, how it communicates success, and how they can be successful in their new role, you will have gone a long way in ensuring that the person doing the work will do a good job. Best of all, you will also be successful.

You will be successful as an entrepreneurial manager because you will feel less inclined to micro-manage. Moreover, you will know your new hire has the knowledge they need to navigate a business world that, up until this point, only you have truly known. They may not know everything you know, but they are off to a good start. They are off to a good start because you have equipped them with the background knowledge necessary to help them help you. Now, if they could only do what you can do.

CHAPTER 6

DO WHAT I DO: THE SECOND FLOOR

MAGGIE WAS A LEADER at an inner-city nonprofit. She had a warm, south-of-London British accent and was always quick with a joke to make people smile. But Maggie had a problem. She had more sales opportunities than she had time. She had so many opportunities, in fact, that she needed to move some nonessential work off her plate. Seeing her immediate team as the quickest answer to her time constraints, she decided to pass the work that she did not want to do down to them. She justified that the team worked for her, and that they would understand the extra work requirements given the great opportunity ahead.

At first, Maggie's teammates were happy to do the work because she was a good person to work for. But over time, some of her wider team became disillusioned with her managerial approach. You see, each person had a specific role to play on her team, and sometimes Maggie gave them work that did not fit within the context of what they were originally hired to do. Maggie did not see this as an issue because she valued time and not roles. After all, she had hired smart people whom she could trust. Besides, she reasoned, when she first started at the nonprofit, she would have happily taken on any kind of work just to keep things moving.

But the sentiment did not carry. Maggie began to get criticism for handing off all sorts of work—work that was not in line with what her team members were originally hired to do. Ultimately this affected her reputation with her colleagues, and worse, her assuming managerial style made it difficult for people to trust her whenever she asked them to take on new work. If Maggie had some reactionary need, then the entire team had to react as well.

Maggie did a great job casting vision, but unfortunately, she thought casting vision would cover all the context switching she put employees through. She failed to recognize that vision is contextual to a person's role. If the work constantly changes, but the vision stays the same, people will feel disconnected and frustrated with their work. This leads to a lack of trust in the employer.

Maggie did not build roles to fit the vision of the business and so roles changed with the whims of the work week. What Maggie needed was a framework that would build the fundamentals of delegation directly into the roles themselves. If she had this framework, she would have been able to model the work she needed her team to do, keep the work focused on the ultimate vision, and recover her time as well.

THE DELEGATION TRIAD

Your new managerial house is built on trust. And the first floor is based on your business's vision. However, once trust is set and vision is in position, it is time to start the practical part of delegation—getting people to do the work. This is where the second floor, *Do What I Do*, comes in. Building trust continues even here. When you delegate, you must not only trust that a hire knows what to do and why it is important, but that they know how to do the work as well.

In the past, you may have done some or even all of the jobs you are now delegating yourself. Or perhaps you did not do the work, and so the business suffered some level of neglect. Either way, you may never have needed to explain how the work gets done—because you were the one who ensured it was done. But now, you need to reverse engineer the work ahead so that someone else can do it for you.

You reverse engineer work (the functions and facts about the role) for your benefit and that of the employee. The exercise builds confidence, and when an employee is confident, you will also be confident in them. The feeling is mutual because the role is both methodically designed and delegated. This is what the second floor is all about—teaching a person they can do what you can do—and be successful too. We gain this confidence through a simple framework called The Triad.

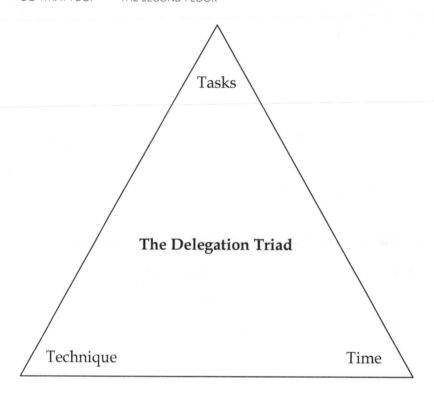

Tasks

The Delegation Triad

Technique

Time

The Triad is made up of three T's. They are tasks, technique, and time. Tasks are the things you do. Technique is how you do them. Time is how long it takes you (or someone else) to accomplish a task with the right technique. Everything about a person's role will come back to tasks, technique, and time. To this point, if you ever have concerns about a person's work, those concerns will also be rooted in one of these three areas. For this reason, we can think of The Triad as the way in which we define the working role of the employee. These three T's are critical, so we will spend the next few chapters unpacking the concept of Do What I Do by constructing your own work triad for a role.

THE GOLDILOCKS GOAL

The Triad will give you clarity on what you will delegate, and thereby, what the employee will do. But there is another benefit as well. It will lower the risk of overworking the new recruit.

Overwork is a big risk for new hires who enter a small business—the risk stems from work that has gone unattended until their arrival. Most entrepreneurs rightfully want to offload unattended work, such as overdue projects, backlogged orders, sales, and the like, to catch up on lost time. But if all this work is delegated too quickly, it overwhelms the role of the employee.

This sets a bad precedent and leads to burnout, which is frustrating for both you and the employee. The good news is that you can prevent the burnout-causing fire from starting.

You see, overworking an employee is the result of one of two things. Either the role is too large, and work gets included that the person cannot do, or the role is too small, and the employee spins their wheels on too much low-value work. By calibrating the role upfront, you keep the lines of work clear, focused, and productive. You want the goldilocks effect—not too much work and not too little.

A role that is too small will have the employee wasting time obsessing over a mountain of details. A role that is too large will find the employee spread too thin. Both scenarios lead to employee burnout, and burnout punishes the employee for problems they did not create.

NOT PART-OWNER

Now, entrepreneurs who are new to management may over-delegate with good intent. The hope here is that the new hire will enthusiastically contribute to the business, gain experience, and simultaneously recover the owner's lost time. Some owners even see an employee's ability to handle these extra requests as a good sign. The thinking stems from the owner's belief that wearing multiple hats is a sign of taking ownership and a promotion-worthy behavior.

The new hire is fresh for the fight, right? In the mind of entrepreneurs who think this way, the employee is now a part-owner of the business's success. In truth, they are not.

The employee's role is just that: a role. Unless the hire has real equity or private stock, the employee does not own anything other than the tasks they have been delegated. So, if you see an employee working extra hard to compensate for newly delegated work, be aware—what may appear as a go-getter attitude is likely just a fear of not meeting expectations. Fears like these can lead an employee to outright quit—that is, if burnout does not get them first.

A new hire needs a narrow lane to be successful in their role. You build this lane with tasks, technique, and time. Let's take a deeper look at tasks—the work your employee will do.

CHAPTER 7

HOW TO CREATE MANAGEABLE TASKS

YEARS AGO, I WORKED FOR AN EXCITING marketing startup. My role on the team was to lead our digital products team—creating big websites and super-niche brands. That is, until upper management decided we should also produce video commercials for them as well. I liked videography and had big respect for people who could do it, but I personally had no experience with leading video or commercial production. I had no choice in the matter, however, and quickly had to channel my inner Spielberg (pre-Jaws era, mind you).

When my role changed, I was stuck doing work I was not qualified to do. Directing films is much different from directing engineers, but the management team seemed to think all creative work was the same. Even though my title never changed, the major theme of my role did. This big change in the business put me in a position where the vision for the business and the vision of my role were in conflict.

Let's assume you have an employee who, thanks to their access of the first floor—Know What I know—has a vision for their new role.

Now that the employee has a vision for their role, they should also have a specific, narrow focus that enables their success. You create this focus with a concept called themes, not the tasks themselves.

TASK THEMES

True to their name, themes determine what type of work an employee will do but not the work itself. Thematic work is very useful because it prevents you from redefining a person's role when the business changes, or perhaps more frequently, you get pressed for time. Task themes define the range and boundaries of assignable tasks, not to mention the amount of agency a person has to make decisions on their own. Thematic work also prevents an employee from feeling as though they are doing busy work or work for which they are unqualified. The first step in defining the right tasks is to define the right themes for those tasks.

THE STRUCTURE OF A THEME

You can think of a theme as a bucket—a bucket that will hold the tasks you will soon delegate to the new role. Practically, a theme outlines the group of work that comprises a *part* of a role.

I recommend keeping a role to no more than 3–5 themes. Any more, and it will be hard to measure the success of an individual's work later on. Worse, you will end up with an employee who is constantly putting out fires they are not equipped to handle. If this happens, the employee will be frustrated about having to put out fires and you will be frustrated that there are fires. Eventually, you will wonder if you made the right decision in hiring them in the first place.

The benefit of thematic work is twofold. First, a theme provides context for the work to be done, and second, a theme will provide clarity on what is out of scope for the role. To this end, a theme is intentionally inclusive of some types of work and exclusive of other types of work.

To create a theme, start by defining a high-level responsibility that is *not* a specific task. Let's review a few examples. Task themes for a data engineer might include the following:

- Due diligence for web services
- Technical analysis
- Systems management

Here is an example of task themes for an administrative assistant:

- Schedule management
- Proof content
- Client management

Notice how the themes in examples are not overly specific. You cannot create a KPI or measurable outcome for the role based on "due diligence" for an engineer, but the theme does tell you the role will not involve contributing to the creative direction of projects or something related to marketing. This is important. We are creating buckets, not collecting drops of water. All we want is a label.

Once you have created a theme's label, define your task themes with a short description. This definition will keep the work from being overly broad. It will also set context when you do list out the tasks to be done.

Here is an example of a theme description:

Theme
Technical Analysis
Description
The team member will evaluate digital products from the perspective of technical feasibility. They will help the business navigate how software is implemented, and to what degree, based on timelines, risks, hardware, and third-party tools available.

Download The Free Template!

Get the **Task Theme** template along with other great tools included with this book at:

https://piercebrantley.co/NYJ-downloads

Note that in our example theme's description, there are clear boundaries for the employee, but you still cannot find any specific, daily tasks. This is what we want. Themes are about the type of work you delegate as much as the specific tasks the person will do. Inversely, themes also define what is not thematic about a role.

MATCHING THEMES TO EXPECTATIONS

A web developer I knew was fired after they fell behind in their work. After reflecting on the reasons for their termination, I noticed their manager had changed the theme of work for which the developer was hired.

In the manager's mind, all coding was "web guru" work. With this perspective in mind, they changed the developer's work from front-end, highly visual, and collaborative work to back-end, database, and systems work.

The developer did their best to keep up with the change in the role but was not equipped to handle their new theme of work. To use an analogy, it was as if the manager had asked them to start speaking

Mandarin when they were an expert in Spanish. The employee simply could not keep up with the new way of working because they could not speak the language.

Most employees want to be accommodating in their role—especially on small teams. But people are not Swiss Army Knives. They need focus to stay sharp. Task themes help prevent dulling, unproductive work from being assigned to good workers. Themes also help you establish healthy boundaries for the type of work you choose to delegate. This creates more focused workers and allows for organic innovation to occur.

In the case of our front-end developer, the person worked very hard and helped the company innovate in a number of ways, but when one of their major themes changed, the frame for their performance changed as well. Where once they produced loads of value for the company, with a new theme, they were an underperformer who fell behind on the job.

At face value, you could assume that this was simply a mismatch of skillset to project need and that the developer's manager simply made a mistake in overextending the role. However, at a deeper level, we find that the business leaders themselves were not concerned with letting organic innovation continue to grow, and instead, were focused on squeezing as much performance as possible from the person doing the work. If they had spent time thinking about where their time should have been focused instead, they would have made room for organic innovation to thrive, because the role's theme would have remained highly focused.

A BENEFIT OF GOOD THEMES

Good themes benefit your time. I always recommend when structuring themes that you think about the time you want to recover. Structure the time you want to recover by removing tasks you should stop doing. Think simply, "What is not my job?"

Once you have your answer, group these removable tasks by theme and use these themes to build the type of work for which an employee will be responsible. Use this new theme as way of creating opportunity for new innovative thinking to occur in your business.

If you want to know more about how to identify work you no longer need to do, you can briefly skip over to the chapter How to Prioritize What You Delegate Next.

A NOTE OF CAUTION FOR THEMES

When you define the type of work a new employee will do, it helps to start with what is out of scope—similar to the way you would with a project or product line. This might seem obvious, but if you do not have a large team, the first thing you will want to do when your time is limited is to hand off the new types of work to an existing employee. Unfortunately, this type of delegation will be detrimental to the quality of the work, not to mention the morale of the employee.

If at some point in the future, you feel strongly that you must give an employee work that was not originally thematic to their role, then first ask them if they feel comfortable taking on the new responsibility. Even if they agree to the work (and you should invite their participation in the decision), be sure to communicate that they will not be evaluated on the normal standards of quality or output to which they are normally held.

ADDING TASKS TO THEMES

Now that you know how to define a theme, you can add in its respective tasks. You build out themes with a task list. Keep the task list straightforward, using actionable language that both you and the hire will understand.

A task list for a theme should be short, no more than 5–7 tasks. This keeps a theme manageable and focused. Let's continue with the example theme we used above. A list of tasks within the theme Technical Analysis might look like this:

- Critique new documentation for APIs.
- Report on gaps in technical understanding.
- Create technical roadmaps for new products.
- Present on IoT research and make suggestions for new projects.

Download The Free Template!

Get the **Task Creation** template along with other great tools included with this book at:

https://piercebrantley.co/NYJ-downloads

As you can see, tasks are the specific work for which your new hire will be responsible. If the role in question was created to free up your own time, it is best to get clear on the things you want to move off your plate by listing those tasks out here as well. Just be sure they are clearly defined within a theme first.

If you struggle to define which tasks you should place in a theme, your theme is either too specific or you need to create a new theme that corresponds to the work. For instance, if a manager adds "develop website" to the theme "technical analysis" or "sprinkler installations" to the theme of "indoor plumbing," then it is a clear sign that a new theme for development or outdoor plumbing might need to be created. From there, you can decide on whether that theme should be assigned to the same employee or not. Once you have created your task list, it is time to make the tasks trackable.

PERFORMANCE

Good work is measurable work. Good tasks are measurable tasks. If a task is not measurable, it should not exist. When we say measurable, we mean the work should be quantifiable.

Does the employee need to make five widgets a week or seven? Should the widgets be blue or gold? How many of the gold widgets should they aim to sell? The employee should know the expectation. Good work is defined by metrics as much as completion.

What if the task is not turnkey, you may ask? For non-repeatable tasks, you should define performance indicators and then lock those indicators to *time blocks*, which we will discuss in the next section. A performance indicator is simply a value that indicates the quality of work being performed.

TYPES OF PERFORMANCE INDICATORS

There are leading indicators of performance and lagging indicators of performance. This means there are things that tell you upfront if work is headed in the right direction. And there are things that, when the work is completed, tell you if the work was performed to a certain standard.

Indicators are not necessarily KPIs, processes, or goals. As far as this book is concerned, they could be any of those things. The important thing is that you know what the indications of performance are and how an employee works toward them. We will go more in-depth into the process of reporting performance in the chapter Tell What You Know—The Third Floor. As you can imagine, the subject of measuring performance deserves its own dedicated chapter. For now, just remember that work should be measurable if it is to be completed to a reasonable standard of excellence. However, for the sake of clarity, I have included a short example to get you started. Consider the hypothetical task of reducing warranty claims for a home painting business. The performance indicator might be "Keep 5-year warranty claims under 10 percent of present-day monthly sales." This is the lagging indicator of performance for painting a residential home. If the percentage of claims exceeds 10 percent, then the issue might be the process of painting, or the quality of workmanship done by the painter you hired. The measurable process, for the leading indicator of "Keep 5-year warranty claims under 10 percent of present-day monthly sales" is simple—whenever you paint a wall, first prime the wall, then add two top coats, and then finish with a protective clear coat. The task is measurably complete if those steps were followed, which supports the measurable performance indicator for the task. Here is what that task breakdown and its performance indicators would look like:

Task
Actively reduce monthly warranty claims.
Measurable Goal
Keep warranty claims below 10 percent of present-day monthly sales.
Leading Indicator
Homes are painted to standard.
Lagging Indicator
Warranty claims are below 10 percent.

Download The Free Template!

Get the **Task Performance** template along with other great tools included with this book at:

https://piercebrantley.co/NYJ-downloads

INCREASING VISIBILITY OF WORK

Increase the visibility of work to see progress. As you can see in the table, the task is anchored to a goal and there is a process and data point to measure the goal against. This makes a task meaningful and allows both you and the employee to have an "apples to apples" conversation about the work being done. Without this structure, you are both left to assumptions about the quality and quantity of the workload in question.

This lack of visibility affected a friend of mine in a personal way. My friend once created a loan for someone close to them but did not feel as though the person to whom they lent money was meeting their loan agreement. This was causing friction in the relationship, and it noticeably irritated my friend. The payment amount agreed on for the loan was about $500 a month. Knowing my friend, I asked if that agreement was being met.

"Well . . . yes," they said, "but I do not *feel* like they are paying me."

"What do you mean you do not feel like it?" I responded.

They had no concrete answer. My friend just had an anxious feeling.

When my friend looked at their bank account, the amount was deposited, every month, like clockwork. But my friend had not been looking at their bank account, so they had mistrust for the person—even though the agreement was being met. Once they looked at the data, they knew their frustration stemmed from anxiety and not reality. The solution, for both parties, was to increase visibility of the agreement so that trust could be maintained.

At the end of the work week, an employee should be able to give a binary answer to whether the time they spent working is creating a return—by completed tasks or working against a specific task. That is not to say every task they are assigned should be done within a week, but the ability to give specific answers about delivery, within a set timeframe, is critical to the employee feeling as though they have meaningfully contributed to the company as a team member.

Measurable tasks also help keep you, the delegator, from relying on your feelings about in-progress work. For instance, if you have a tendency to get anxious when you do not see someone doing work, a measurable list of tasks will help move you out of the realm of feeling and into that of function.

THE BORING STUFF

A final note on smaller tasks: many roles have low-level work that does not fit neatly into a theme or discipline. These might be tasks like turning in timesheets, locking the office doors when closing, wiping the counter when customers leave, yada yada (Seinfeld voice).

These important but menial tasks can normally be codified into checklists and will end up being part of the training you deliver during onboarding. If the work is detailed, iterative, and specific to the culture of your business, consider making it a checklist that the employee can hang in their office or memorize. This keeps thematic work more role-centric while also helping you develop processes for normal, low-level work which needs to be done for the business to run smoothly.

When you structure a role around themes instead of an ever-changing list of tasks, you create a rich and meaningful work experience for your employee. Your business also benefits from the focused work of the employee. Focused employees make for a focused business. A focused business allows your time to be free for what is most important to your entrepreneurial endeavors. Once you know the work an employee will do, you can shift to how they do it.

CHAPTER 8

HOW TO TEACH AND TRAIN A NEW HIRE

AS A KID, I WORKED FOR A LOCAL FARM, harvesting potatoes out in the boondocks of East Texas. I bet you did not know ETX was prime potato country, but it is—or at least, it was. I had that job for a day. On that day, the farmer took me out to his potato garden, gave me a sturdy hoe, and told me to spend my time filling up a nearby wheelbarrow with all the starchy gold I could find. The only problem was, he never told me how delicate potatoes are when they cannot see the quick swing of a thirteen-year-old farmhand.

After the farmer left, I quickly got to work. My first swing cut straight through a plant and sliced a buried potato in half. The potato was really big, however, so I figured it was already too large for the market. But that was only the first causality.

By the time I had finished, nearly half the potatoes were destroyed because my hoe hand was too strong, the potatoes were too big, or the stupid plants had just decided to grow outside the reasonable lines of the plotted row. To even the score, I threw a bunch of the fry-bait in the nearby forest.

The farmer, however, had a near Rain Man ability for counting his crop and knew I made a mistake.

In disgrace, I gave back the hoe, hung up my career as a potato farmer, and bought some french fries with the twelve dollars I earned from cultivating the land. I can only wonder what my life would have looked like if I had been taught how to harvest potatoes correctly.

GOOD TECHNIQUE

Proper technique is all about doing a job successfully. You can delegate all the right tasks, with all the right themes, and someone may still fail in their role if the way they work does not work for you or the goals of your company. This is why training is so important at the onset of someone starting their job.

You have a decision to make. People can either do work the way you want them to or the way they should. Sometimes this is the same thing. Sometimes it is not.

Here is how you know the difference. You want people to work just like you if the values of your company lead people to work in a way that is different from the rest of your industry. However, if you are in a mature market, have little understanding of the work, or compete in a space that is highly regulated, you may do better to simply hire people who value doing things the way they are normally done. You can either hire an expert or foster expert-level thinking.

HIRING AN EXPERT

How do you know which direction you should go? One way to start is to honestly evaluate your own expertise for the role in which you are hiring.

For example, let's say you need to hire a social media manager for your business. Up until this point, you have done all the posting yourself. Perhaps you have read a couple of articles on social media engagement and even attended some training, but if you are honest, your TikTok following should really be higher for the type of business you run.

In this scenario, you need to say, "not my job," and trust the person you are hiring to do what they do best. Unless your business is focused on your celebrity, your ultimate role is not to be an influencer. Any time you spend trying to go viral just detracts from your role as an entrepreneurial manager. Training proper technique, for this hire, should be focused on how they integrate with the existing business in a meaningful way.

FOSTER EXPERT-LEVEL DIFFERENTIATION

On the other hand, if the values of your business somehow drive the way in which people work, then you should, in fact, mold a person's approach to work in way that helps the business differentiate itself in the market.

One of my favorite examples of this is with Favor, the food delivery service. Favor is my favorite way to order food and I will tell you why—they talk to me like I am a real person. From the onset of the last-mile wars, I preferred their approach to delivery because every time I ordered, the person who delivered my meal communicated to me in the exact same way as the last person I interacted with at Favor. Every conversation on the platform is optimistic, timely, and keeps me in the loop about every detail of the ordering process. Perhaps they are a little emoji happy, but who does not like a unicorn with their tacos?

If the founders of Favor simply wanted to meet industry standards, they could have done something similar to the Pizza Hut app tracker and called it a day. But they seem to understand that, in their business, good interactions equal steady traction. Somehow this value comes through in their approach to communication on the platform.

If you are hiring someone who comes with an existing skillset, consider how the values of your business might shape the way in which people work. How do those values of yours change the way a person would normally do their job at your business as compared to somewhere else? How will you communicate this to them early in the training process?

TWO APPROACHES FOR GUIDING TRAINING ON PROPER TECHNIQUE

There are two ways in which you can guide a new hire to work in your business. The first method is shadowing. The second is training. Shadowing is simple but comes with pitfalls and is time intensive for you. Formal training is thorough but often requires your business to have standard operating procedures already in place. More often than not, you will use a blend of both approaches.

If your new hire is already an expert, your training will focus more on values and team integration. If your new hire is learning from you directly, you will focus more on the way in which you have personally done the work in the past. Let's look at each approach in a little more detail to discover how they can help you equip an employee.

SHADOWING

Shadowing is a type of unstructured, learn-by-doing training that is designed to immerse someone in your particular way of working. Shadowing is scrappy. The approach involves learning by observation and discovery. A lot of entrepreneurs choose this approach because they lack time to put something more formal in place.

When someone shadows you, you are the guardrail, and the work is the bowling alley. The new hire is the ball, doing their best to hit strikes for the company. They will be in your shadow, so to speak, until you feel comfortable with their scoring record.

Shadowing is simple—it's watch and learn, then ask and try. Once the initial onboarding is complete, simply have the new hire watch you do their tasks for a set period of time. Continue to do their job as you would have before they joined, allowing them to watch you work and ask as many questions as possible. Repeat the process with their particular set of task themes until you feel comfortable with their performance.

One added benefit of this approach is that it can also help you refine the tasks and task themes for which the hire will be responsible. As an employee shadows you, you may discover new details about certain tasks that have big impacts on the final performance of the work. You would not have discovered the importance of the details without the hire asking questions and observing how they do the work themselves. Teaching is learning twice, as they say.

You can use these new findings to create training documentation and catalog common Q&As. Hopefully, with the next employee, there will be less shadowing and more effective training as a result.

While shadowing is effective, it will require a steep time commitment from you. This is because this approach is primarily a show-and-tell exercise. Because it is so time intensive, it may present a problem if you discover you do not have enough time to give your new hire—which can frustrate both of you. This frustration, spurred by your lack of availability, may lead you to simply tell the employee to figure out the work themselves. If this happens, the process of training is never completed and may result in haphazard work on the part of the new employee.

BUDGETING TIME FOR SHADOW-TRAINING

If you choose the shadow-training approach, budget some of your time exclusively for the hire's learning. During this dedicated time, do not schedule meetings, take sales calls, or work on new projects unless the individual might benefit from being included in them. If you do not budget time for shadow-training, you will simply defer the risk of low-quality work to some point in the future.

While it may not seem like a big deal to take a break to deal with some pressing issue, the break in learning will affect the employee's retention of information. Even worse, the pause in learning may lead them to think you will not be present for them when they do have an issue that needs your attention.

All this said, shadowing as a form of training can be an effective way to build trust and rapport with a new employee. If you do choose to let someone shadow you, make sure to set an end date in mind when they own the work themselves. The duration of time should depend on how valuable or risk-prone you consider the new hire's role to be.

With this approach, you can always choose to gradually taper off your role in the work, slowly letting go of old responsibilities until you feel fully comfortable with the work being done. Just be sure to communicate that this is your intention if the employee is to shadow you for an extended period of time.

FORMAL TRAINING

Training is a structured approach to learning how to do work while on the job. The best training is a mix of knowledge transfer from you and practical, hands-on work. To this end, it is a good idea to split your formal training process between whiteboard learning and hands-on learning. This blended approach to training will help the hire absorb head knowledge and useful kinesthetic training.

Once you determine what you want them to know, blend these two types of learning into a structure that models what a typical day will look like for an employee. By modeling training around the employee's typical day, you help them build a mental model for how they will show up to work. Consider this example of someone whose job is to make sales calls:

Whiteboard Knowledge

- Why is the product they are selling important?
- Who needs the product?
- How the product fits into the company's mission?
- Learn the sales process.

- Learn the sales script.

- Memorize and define sales goals.

Kinesthetic Training

- Practice 10 sales calls.

- Meet with marketing about lead gen process.

- Watch a senior salesperson follow up with a lead.

- Record the number of calls made during a day.

Notice how these two categories of learning separate the why and how from the what and when. The whiteboard knowledge is focused on business goals, while the kinesthetic training is focused on the daily grind.

Before you conduct any training, spend some time thinking through what the employee needs to know before you can set them loose at work. Consider what head knowledge will benefit them as well as where they might need to spend some extra time practicing in order to feel confident in their new role. If the employee is the one bringing expertise, consider asking them where they have seen bottlenecks before regarding the types of work you are asking them to do.

Before you host a training workshop for the employee, download the training template worksheet to help you make a plan. And if you really want to ace the training, spend some time doing a dry run before you host the training session to see if any gaps come up that you may have missed in the planning process.

Download The Free Template!

Get the **Onboarding Workshop** template along with other great

tools included with this book at:

https://piercebrantley.co/NYJ-downloads

Every business, yours included, will have its own way to conduct training, but every business should develop training as a step within the onboarding process. Remember, the goal of training is to set up your new hire for success so that you can recover your time. To the extent you train, mistakes are limited.

MISTAKES: PART OF THE TRAINING PROCESS

As with anything new, it is good to assume you will see a reasonable number of mistakes, questions, and even some short-term losses as the hire gets comfortable in their new role. For some entrepreneurs, this can be difficult to stomach—especially if they know exactly how the work should be done. In these scenarios, I have even seen managers remind their new employees that they are "taking a risk" by hiring them, telling them that any potential mistakes will cost the business money. Obviously, this risk should be calculated by the employer and should not be mentioned to the employee.

Any mistakes or short-term loss you incur during the period of onboarding is negligible compared to the unrealized gains you won't be able to claim without the new hire's help. If the idea of losses makes you feel uncomfortable, consider that the new hire is taking a risk on you, your business, and their livelihood by choosing to work with you. They could work with anyone, at any business, but they are willing to give you their time. There is a mutual, win-win exchange and the risk is equal for both of you.

If you do see a lot of mistakes that continue for more than ninety days, then you might need to reevaluate your hiring decision, or better yet, the sophistication of your training process. Until then, assume there will be a reasonable number of mistakes and losses, and be pleasantly surprised when they do not occur. Better yet, bake it into your hiring budget. Both you and the hire will feel less pressure, and the quality of work will likely be higher as well. You can always come back and further reduce any anxiety with additional training.

TRAINING FOR FUTURE SUCCESS

No matter how you choose to train an employee, you want to ensure you are not putting your business in maintenance mode by the way you teach them to work.

Here's what I mean. In the past, the process of delegating was all about getting a predictable outcome from an employee. The goal of this old form of delegating was to prize predictability over everything else. Predictability is good. You cannot plan without it, but if everyone you train thinks like a burger flipper, then you are building a franchise. Franchise thinking puts guardrails up in the mind of the employee and stifles the possibility of organic innovation from taking root in your business. It puts your business in maintenance mode. The secondary effect of this type of thinking is that the employee does not feel like their potential can grow at the same clip as the business for which they work.

As an entrepreneurial manager, the key is to remember that the work this employee does no longer belongs to you. Of course, you want to guide them and help them succeed in their role, but you do not want to be so heavy handed in your training that you eliminate the potential for new ideas or ways of doing things. Entrepreneurs who overemphasize the methods for the way work gets done will find that they have chosen to invest in their business yet limit their potential return. Train for success, but make room for organic innovation. Once you have established your ideal path for training, you can focus on the time it takes to get stuff done.

CHAPTER 9

HOW TO MANAGE AN EMPLOYEE'S TIME

"I'M GONNA PUNT THAT ONE!" said the engineer.

Yes. That's the enthusiasm we've been missing, I thought. I could have spun a pen around my finger, Gordon Gecko style, I was so pleased.

But then I noticed something odd. Every so often, as we moved through the list of milestones in our planning meeting, the engineer would continue to quip, "Gonna punt that one, too!" Each time they said this little phrase, I sensed their enthusiasm drop, so I decided to pry.

"When you say punt . . . I guess that means you are going to really knock it out of the park?" I maintained an even tone, hoping they would not notice I mixed sports metaphors.

"Ah, no . . ." they responded. "It means I am going to kick it down the line. I don't see the value in some of these little tasks, and I think things will be fine if I skip them for now. We will pick them up at some point in the future."

I was stunned. In what world did they think that was okay?

But they continued, "Really, it all comes down to time. I want to get this project done quickly, and I think some of this stuff will slow us down." Their response sounded reasonable, but one task, in particular, seemed pretty small—about two hours of work.

"What about adding this list to the website?" I asked.

"Oh, gosh . . . three weeks at least," they responded. There was no way—three weeks was basically the whole project! With all that extra time, they could have caught half the "punts" they sent down the line. Clearly, we needed to set some expectations for how long the work should take to complete.

TIME MANAGEMENT = BUSINESS MANAGEMENT

Time is the last component of The Triad. If tasks tell the hire what they will do, and technique tells them how they will do it, then time is what informs them of the speed at which the work should be done. Time alone will help you measure the effectiveness of someone's work against the pace of your business goals.

Unlike our project-punting colleague, most employees like to be held to a reasonable standard of excellence. I say reasonable because employees want to perform well against expectations, but they also want those expectations to be realistic compared to the complexity and pace of work. You will set these expectations with time blocks— a special unit of time that will help you predict and measure task-specific work.

MEASURING TIME AND AVOIDING TIME BIAS

In order to effectively measure the amount of time an employee spends on work, each task you delegate should be paired with a custom time block. A time block is a unit of time particular to a type of task. It sets a benchmark for how long tasks within a theme of work should take to complete. To this end, a time block will serve as a guide for you to measure how effective and efficient a person is at a particular task.

Time blocks are particularly useful if you used to do the work yourself or have some familiarity with the person's role. If this sounds like you, I have some tough news—you likely underestimate the true amount of time it takes to complete someone else's task. We call this perspective a time bias. A time bias is a subconscious program that runs in your brain. When it is operating, the time bias underestimates the amount of time it takes to get work done.

An entrepreneurial manager, I knew was frequently frustrated with people because of a time bias. Their story demonstrates why all of us need to be aware of how they time bias spring up. In this case, the entrepreneur's bias started when they moved out of their role as an engineer. At first, they were excited about the transition. They sensed the importance of their new role and decided to hire a project manager as well as a few engineers to replace the work they used to do. But unbeknownst to them, they operated under the assumption that they were quicker than average at their work.

On calls, the manager was quick to pontificate about how they could do tasks that would normally take someone a few days in as little as an hour or so. In their mind, an engineer who was fully devoted to development should be able to get 5x the amount of work done as they previously used to do.

However, when I observed the manager doing their old job, they would often take days to solve problems that they said would only take a couple of hours. When asked about why a particular task took them longer than they thought it should, they would offer up reasons for why they got bogged down in meetings or had things come up that blocked their work. When they were pressed for a deeper explanation, they would still hold that they were faster than the actual proof held true. Their time bias was so bad that it ended up affecting the project manager's ability to plan effectively.

AVOIDING POOR PLANNING

Entrepreneurial managers who have unrealistic ideas about time management are caught in a phenomenon called the Planning Fallacy. The Planning Fallacy was first proposed by psychologist Daniel Kahneman in the late 1970s. In his research, Kahneman discovered a phenomenon that shed light on how we all tend to incorrectly predict the amount of time we need to complete our work. For managers, it works like this: those who are caught in this phenomenon tend to hold an optimistic bias toward the work they do. Meaning, that they underestimate the real amount of time required to complete a task.

I believe the reasons for this type of underestimate go back to the Antivalues to which we hold. If our identity is somehow connected to performance, our mind will frame us in the best possible light. All entrepreneurial managers can get caught in Kahneman's Planning Fallacy, but in my experience, those who are new to delegating are most prone. The reason? New entrepreneurs often know how to do some aspect of the work they are about to delegate.

EXPERTISE AND GOOD ESTIMATES

Expertise does not necessarily make for better times estimates. In fact, expertise can make an estimate worse because it typically comes with experience—an experience that may make the expert faster than average. But the Planning Fallacy occurs regardless of an individual's experience. Just like the technical manager mentioned earlier, most of us just plain suck at estimating the time it takes to complete work.

The data around the guesswork of work is also astounding. In "It's About Time: Optimistic Predictions in Work and Love," a paper written by Roger Buehler, Dale Griffin, and Michael Ross, we learn that the likelihood of someone both estimating and achieving a certain task in the right amount of time is about 45 percent.

So, what is the lesson here? Most of the time, your best estimates are wrong. If you think a task will take four hours to complete, you will be right less than half of the time. In reality, the task will likely take much longer.

MY KINGDOM FOR A STOPWATCH

Without an outside standard, the effects of time bias are very hard to shake. In our example, the technical manager assumed their most difficult tasks only took about two hours to complete, when, they actually took about three days to complete. Their project manager proved this point when they crafted a plan for new developers.

Even though the workday was eight hours, there were only about 4–5 hours of focused task time in the business. The rest of the time was spent at planning meetings, lunch, and team exercises. This was the same type of day the previous engineer, now manager, used to have. In reality, the tasks really did take about three days. We discovered the true amount of time the work would take because the project manager knew how to use data to avoid time bias.

Ironically, the manager still did not believe the project manager when they were shown the data. Do not be that manager. Your employees will thank you for being realistic about the length of time it takes. They might even work hard to try and beat the status quo.

You do not need a certified project manager, however, to accurately predict and measure the time it takes for someone to do their work. You just need unbiased standards e.g., *time blocks,* to get good at predicting the general amount of time it takes for an employee to do different kinds of work.

There are three simple time-blocking tools you can use to help you get accurate time management predictions:

Personal experience benchmarks give you a quick and easy way to discover how long a certain type of work will take. Here, you set the benchmark. Just try not to cheat.

Industry standards have historical precedence in the industry. In other words, the industry is known for doing a certain type of work at a certain pace.

Quantity-to-Clock ratio is a straightforward metric that depends on the number of units or tasks done in a specific time period.

Let's look at each approach in a little more detail. Afterward, you can decide on the right approach for your business and the role at hand.

PERSONAL EXPERIENCE BENCHMARK

Personal Experience Benchmarks (PEBs) are useful for first-time managers who are familiar with how to do the work they are choosing to delegate. PEBs are useful because you do not need to think too deeply about what the exact standard should be. You simply need to record yourself doing the work as it will be delegated. Because you are the expert, your pace serves an aspirational standard. The exercise might even be enlightening if you have never confronted a time bias in your own work.

How do you know if you should use a PEB versus one of the other time-blocking tools? This time block is best used for less repetitive tasks that are *unique* to your business and take a medium-to-high level of expertise to do. If a task does not fit these criteria, move to the next two options, Industry Standard and Quantity-to-Clock Ratio.

To create a PEB, first choose a task within one of the themes of work you previously defined. Complete the task yourself, at a normal pace, and use a timer or stopwatch to record the amount of time it takes you to complete the task. If the task ranges in difficulty, record the amount of time it takes at varying ranges of difficulty, and then take the average of all the times. This average will serve as a benchmark—the generally accepted amount of time it requires a person to do the task. If a task has a very wide range of difficulty, take the average of a set of tasks with the standard of difficulty that is unique to your business. I like to recommend taking the average of about five iterations of a task, respective to its particular level of complexity.

For PEBs that take a lot of time, such as a phase of a construction project or financial planning, try to reference your business's historical performance to create a benchmark. If the task is highly technical or requires a lot of training in a specialized technique, then set a reasonable amount of time for a person to work up to this benchmark. Remember, if the person comes with no experience, they will not initially hit your PEB.

NO HIGH SCORES

A PEB is tied to your performance, and because of this, you may find yourself rushing faster than you normally would to hit a personal best with your time. Resist this urge. Your business is not an arcade (unless it is), and your high score does not help the employee.

There are a couple of reasons why setting a personal best is counterproductive when you benchmark. The first reason is that you will subconsciously revert to putting your identity in the work—work of which you are now free. You no longer achieve work; you guide work. Doubling down on a personal best is counterproductive. You create a PEB to move out of dataless assumptions about how long it takes to do things. Hopefully, your recruit will soon surpass your benchmarks standards anyway.

The second reason is morale. An employee does not need to know they are working against your personal best. Why? An employee who spends their time competing to beat your personal best deviates their energy from doing good work to trying to simply impress you. This can lead to slips in quality and puts them in a poor frame of mind. To this end, if you create a PEB, just frame it as a business standard: "Our goal at [Insert Business] is to complete the work within [Insert Time Length]." When you present a PEB as a business standard, it keeps insecurity from creeping into the work and can even give the employee ownership in a bigger company goal.

INDUSTRY STANDARDS

Hand-washing a car takes two hours to complete. Unloading a fishing boat takes 45 minutes. Creating a blueprint for an 1,800-square foot house takes three business weeks. Industry standards are like PEBs, but they differ in that there is an existing precedent for all businesses like yours—the employee just may not know it yet. Ford, for instance, has been said to send a completed F-150 truck down the factory line about once every minute. But this speed is predicated on a truck taking approximately 20 hours to build.

Every person on the factory floor has specific time allotments to get their job done. If one person goes too slow, the effect is felt all the way down the line. Industry standards like these set a precedent for the competitiveness of your business. Use industry standards when your customers and your competition already have expectations about how long something should take. This approach will help an employee meet the existing mark of delivery.

Another important reason to use industry standards is if you are managing a role where you do not completely understand the work. With an established outside standard, you will know with reasonable certainty whether the work is getting done in a reasonable amount of time. Just be sure to understand the potential risk factors associated with the standard so that you do not set unrealistic expectations.

QUANTITY-TO-CLOCK RATIO

Lastly, we have Quantity-to-Clock ratios. QtCs are when you simply need a certain number of repetitive tasks done in a set amount of time. Use this type of time measurement when you have turnkey, assembly-line type work. QtCs are useful when you need to get a certain number of units or services done in a strict amount of time. QtCs are best used when the tasks are very small, and repetitive (think of Lucille Ball, on the show *I Love Lucy*, checking chocolates on the assembly line).

QtCs are built like this. First, define the amount of time an employee should spend doing a task each day or week. This is the time budgeted for the task theme, not how long it takes someone to do the task. Second, define how many times the tasks should be completed within the time you budgeted for the task theme.

For instance, let's say you own a car wash, and you want six hours a day to be spent washing cars. Your new employee will only focus on standard detailing jobs, and you want them to do eight each day. In this example, this task has a 3:4 ratio, and each car detail should take 45 minutes.

The higher the right-side consequent term is, the more efficient you expect the employee to be at their job. You can also use a QtC as way to measure performance and use it in reports as well.

PUT IT TOGETHER WITH TIME TEMPLATES

Once you have decided on the best way to benchmark and measure performance for the tasks an employee will do, you can build out a type of calendar, called a time template, for the employee to work against.

In some businesses, this approach might feel rigid. Although, entrepreneurs who feel this way are often not great at time management themselves. I concede that not everything in a business works like clockwork, but for roles that typically do routine work, it is often helpful to have a time template for reference. The reason goes back to the values discussion we had earlier.

If you value your time and know where your business needs focused energy, then building out a time template can help you visualize where an employee spends their time. You can then reference this document if you feel that the business's performance is slipping, or you sense the employee is focusing on things that are not conducive to their role. As an operations exercise, they also serve as helpful playing cards to determine how you might divide a person's time. Here is an example of a time template:

Role			
Junior Car Wash Crew			
Days Assigned	**Task**	**Time block Type**	**Task Theme**
M, T, W	Sedan Car Details	QtC	Car Details
Benchmark		**Percentage of Week**	
3:4, 8 car details, 45 minutes each		60 percent	

> ## Download The Free Template!
>
> Get the **Task Time Management** template along with other great tools included with this book at:
>
> https://piercebrantley.co/NYJ-downloads

For roles that are highly structured, I recommend going through each set of task themes and creating playing cards for each task. This will help you plan for future hires and continue to optimize the role as you make adjustments to your business.

A FINAL THOUGHT ON TIME MANAGEMENT

New entrepreneurial managers sometimes feel pressure to be lax on their time management requirements. They may not want to hold the employee to a standard because they do not want to upset them, they want to build rapport, or they consider themselves more easygoing and do not see the need to be too strict. I like to call this Michael Scott Syndrome. It is a serious condition, most notably characterized in the sitcom, *The Office*.

A manager I knew suffered from a chronic case of MSS. The manager, like the one on TV, wanted—needed—the employees to be their friends. The manager often said it was very important for employees to come to them with personal issues or call them after work if they had trouble outside of the workplace. This manager's heart was in the right place, but it deeply affected their ability to manage their employee's time effectively.

While this friendly inclination is well-intentioned, the business and the employee relationship suffer when time and work are not the primary focus of the working relationship.

You see, realistic time expectations have a benefit beyond that of good people management. When an employee can sense you do not have realistic expectations for time management, they may start to sandbag their work. Sandbagging goes by many names, but essentially it means that a once dutiful worker may begin to extend their estimates of how long it takes to get work done. They do this out of self-preservation, not laziness.

The friendly manager mentioned earlier was also known to become erratic when there was pressing work to be done.

On one occasion, an employee stayed up until 2 a.m. to try to complete an urgent project. The next morning, they boasted about their efforts to the manager but let them know there was still more work to be done.

"Did I say stop at two a.m. or stop when the work was completed?" The manager barked. The manager was frustrated that the work was not finished, but they were likely even more frustrated that their friendship with the employee did not compensate for the bad project estimation. The manager's hope was that their relationship would have led the employee to work through the night.

When the working relationship is skewed by a lack of clear expectations, you break trust with employees and open yourself up to sandbagging.

SANDBAGGING

Sandbagging is usually an owner issue. It does not normally happen all at once. Sandbagging is normally the outcome of a lack of trust in you, the manager, accrued over a period of time. It is something that starts because good time blocks are not set at the beginning of the working relationship.

If sandbagging becomes a pattern, it will result in both you and the employee distrusting each other. On one side, you will begin to question their work ethic, and on the other side, they begin to question your ability to manage the business. This can cause a domino effect where you replace a worker, hiring someone else, only to find the process repeating itself indefinitely—which results in your thinking that you can never find good help. Help yourself and set realistic time blocks from the very beginning of the delegating process. You will save yourself and everyone else headaches down the road.

One final point on technique and peace of mind: there is a subtle difference between management and delegation. Delegation is primarily concerned with moving work off your plate and onto someone else's, so you can recover your time for what is most important. Management is primarily concerned with maintaining movement toward a goal, with the help of other people. Delegation and management do overlap. Where the two differ, however, is when you personally have no experience in a new role.

Experienced managers do not need to know how to do the work of the people they are managing. They are managing outcomes and output, not technique and acumen. That is not to say that knowing how to do the work of those you manage is not helpful; it is just not necessary if you are comfortable managing from data and performance indicators.

If you have no real experience in the role for which you are hiring, you can still delegate a responsibility to someone, but you should not fully inform the way in which a certain role is done. If you are not comfortable with the idea of not informing the way in which someone's work is done, then you need to find a manager who has experience doing the work so that they can manage for you. Hiring this middle manager will give you peace of mind when you cannot practically inform someone's approach to the work.

What you *can* always inform, however, are the results you expect to see from the person to whom you are delegating work. If you do not see the results you expect from the person in question, then your role is that of a coach—helping the individual discover the right technique or methodology for their work, based on the measurable outcomes you have set for a particular task. If you hire the right person, you should not have to do this often.

The mechanics of delegation are built on the mastery of tasks, technique, and time. When you combine all three, you will find delegation becomes a habit that is nearly intuitive. And once delegation is intuitive, you can trust that the person doing the work will actually know more about the day to day work than you do. You will be primed and ready to move them to the next floor: Tell What You Know.

CHAPTER 10

TELL WHAT YOU KNOW: THE THIRD FLOOR

THERE I WAS AGAIN, STARING AT THE SCREEN of a highly complex time-management system. It was no Lamborghini, but the software was a custom build. My job, however, as an employee, was to record every task I did during the day, from emails to sales meetings to graphic design in that hulking machine. For each task, I had to record the amount of time I spent doing the work. Whenever I finished a task, I had to enter a new task, and the process would start over. The record-keeping was grueling, almost more tedious than my job.

The company that made the monstrosity thought of management the same way an attorney thinks of defense. If an email was said to be sent, management might ask to read it—just to be sure I was not bluffing. The same was true of sales meetings. If I said I was in a sales meeting in the software, they might call up the client just to be sure it went as I said. The style of management was overbearing, but it was a symptom of management's need to know that the work was done the way they would have done it themselves. If they had known how to implement good reporting, they would have saved everyone from the kind of pain only Microsoft Excel truly knows how to inflict.

You may never dream of asking someone to record every detail of their day—not you, never. However, if you do not have a better way to know if someone is doing their work, you may still regress to over-managing an employee. This type of over-management, through details instead of delegation, will cause an employee to lack ownership in their work.

Employee ownership, as far as this book is concerned, is defined as an employee's ability to execute their tasks, with the right technique, within a time specified. Employees should grow in ownership of their role by executing the precedent set within the delegation triad you are developing.

For most roles, you should be able to see personal ownership on the part of the employee after about a month of regular work. This means, after a month, you should not be involved in their day to day work. Instead, you should be enjoying your newly recovered time.

But an employee who takes full ownership of their work will create a new problem. Good ownership requires good reporting. Good reporting requires that you only know information which moves the needle in your business. To this end, reporting is meant to help you understand the outcomes of work but without the noise of details.

Where details used to make you competent, now they make you cloudy. They prevent you from seeing the big picture.

This is what Tell What You Know is all about. You and your employee now have access to the third floor of The Elevator Effect. As such, you have taken two meaningful ascensions away from doing work in your business. Now it is time to really level up and move toward a more data-driven approach to the work done in your business. On the third floor, you value insight over oversight.

When you simply oversee work, you are heavily involved in the details of the work being done. You are watching the work for accuracy and commitment. While oversight is a necessity at the onset of hiring, oversight should drop off in favor of insight-based management once you are confident in a person's ability to do the work. When you manage from insight instead of oversight, you acknowledge the person who does the work is best equipped to inform how they should work.

For many entrepreneurial managers, the principles of the third floor can be the most difficult to master. This is because it requires that you truly leverage the knowledge of other people instead of your own, historical context for the business. This requires a shift in thinking. The business is no longer just yours—the business is co-owned, at least in terms of work, by everyone who contributes to its success. For this reason, the business no longer rises or falls solely on your decisions and work but also on others who do the work.

Because of this shift, your trust of people should now begin to morph into respect as well, and respect starts with good reporting.

In other words, good reporting shows respect for the individual doing the work.

THE THREE F'S

There are three things that define a reporting system. The elements are 3F's, and are as follows: Frequency, Facts, and Forecasting. Each element helps build a comprehensive picture of the quality of work being done by your employees. A summary of each element is below.

FREQUENCY

Frequency focuses on how often you meet with an employee to review work. The frequency is set by you, the manager, and should be tied to the needs of the business and the level of maintenance the working relationship needs to stay healthy. Reporting frequency is set by the pace of the business—it could be weekly, monthly, quarterly or some combination of all three.

FACTS

Facts are concerned with output and performance of the role. This aspect of reporting is concerned with tactical details. Performance-oriented facts that are meant to showcase the degree to which an employee is hitting their benchmarks.

FORECASTING

Forecasting is all about future performance. Forecasting is a discussion about the future and health of ongoing work based on what you and the employee know today (at the time of meeting). To this end, forecasting is concerned with new opportunities, risks, and areas for improvement as it relates to the employee's role and output at the time of reporting.

A good reporting structure will build rapport with your employee. It will also keep them accountable for the work to which they have been assigned. Some entrepreneurs think creating and listening to reports is a waste of time. They feel it detracts from time spent doing work and replaces it with talking about work. Reporting may feel like a waste of time, but when it's done right, it prevents the waste of time. Many misunderstandings and project risks can be avoided by simply implementing an easy-to-follow reporting system.

When you combine frequency, facts, and forecasting together, you get a complete view of an employee's performance. Best of all, it will be easy for you to understand and for the employee to report on. For this reason, it is in your best interest to spend some time defining what reporting looks like at the onset of creating the role itself.

Let's unpack each element in more detail so you can build out a reporting system that supports your own managerial style.

ON FREQUENCY

Frequency is not just about how often you meet—although you should meet at regular intervals with your employee. Frequency is a tool for business clarity. Business clarity is a lens you build—a lens through which you see your business.

Now that you have stepped away from the work, you will need a range of different perspectives to inform the way you want to see your business. Different types of reports and reporting frequencies will give you different information based on the lens you are looking through.

For example, a quarterly reporting meeting is a bit like looking at your business through the Hubble telescope. You want to see the big picture of the cosmos in its expanse. You are concerned with grander changes in your universe. Monthly meetings are like looking at the moon through the Griffith Observatory in Los Angeles, California. In this type of meeting, you want to understand worlds you are familiar with but ultimately removed from. And lastly, something like a weekly report is like looking at details through a microscope. You are studying something in its complexity to understand minute shifts in structure and evolution.

There is no right way to set up how often you require reports to be given. But the anatomy of your reporting structure should give you a full view of your universe, encompassing future changes, the big picture, and the important details.

Some managers like to set up reporting from the onset of hiring. Other managers may wait until they feel like they are losing touch with the important details of their business. Ultimately, you should implement a reporting structure once you can trust someone to do the work they were hired for without your direct supervision.

WAITING FOR REPORTING

However, if you do wait too long for reporting to begin, you may feel the urge to step in when some new risk is introduced—even though the employee can very likely handle even the riskiest situations in their work world. Managers who control work reactively are almost always operating with half the data they need to make informed decisions. It goes without saying, that a manager who regularly jumps in to solve problems without the right information will find themselves with a greater problem—the employee will eventually quit because they aren't trusted.

Set up a reporting structure as early as necessary to prevent poor performance. You will avoid all sorts of problems and save yourself stress, gray hair, and bottles of cheap vodka—unless cheap vodka is your thing—but even if it is, you should set up regular times to meet with your direct report.

HOW TO DEFINE REPORTING FREQUENCY

Decide how often you want to meet and why. Make the meeting formal and do your best to not have them during lunch or other casual time. Your goal is to digest facts and understand the health of your business. You are like a doctor. The checkup may be routine, but both you and the employee care very much about the reality of the facts. Focused time will focus the details of the conversation. Below are some examples of how to structure different types of reporting meetings.

DAILY MEETING

Meeting Type: Daily Report

When: Every day at 9:00 a.m.

Goal: The goal of the daily report is to communicate what will be accomplished during the day along with expected outputs, and to solve any risks or blockers that may be present before the work begins.

Meeting Length: 20 Minutes

WEEKLY MEETING

Meeting Type: Weekly Report

When: Every Friday at 11:30 a.m.

Goal: The goal of the weekly report is to understand how many new accounts were closed, which clients have yet to sign their contracts, and any risks or wins accrued in the last week.

Meeting Length: 1 hour

MONTHLY MEETING

Meeting Type: Monthly Report

When: Last Wednesday of the month at 3 p.m.

Goal: The goal of the monthly report is to review project progress and output goals as they relate to benchmarks and discuss readiness for the next month.

Meeting Length: 2 hours

QUARTERLY MEETING

Meeting Type: Quarterly Report

When: Last Monday of the quarter at 9:00 a.m.

Goal: The goal of the quarterly report is to understand the health of the business and how past work has contributed to the efficiency and revenue of the business. Decide on new goals, and review our biggest wins and losses.

Meeting Length: 2 hours

ANNUAL MEETING

Meeting Type: Annual Report

When: Last Friday of the year at 9:00 a.m.

Goal: The goal of the annual report is to review the year's wins and losses and plan for new growth and efficiencies for the next year.

Meeting Length: 5 hours

Download The Free Template!

Get the **Reporting Meeting** template along with other great tools included with this book at:

https://piercebrantley.co/NYJ-downloads

Once you have set the frequency of your reporting, you can focus on the information you want to know when you meet with your employee.

ON FACTS

In management, facts are the foundation of trust—and trust is the means and measure by which you delegate. You want to trust that your employee is working on the right things, and your employee wants you to trust that they know what they are doing. In the end, good reporting all comes down to the type of information you want to receive when a report is due.

I have known some managers who only wanted high-level details that corresponded to a project. I have also seen managers ask their employees to plot out how client relationships were progressing on highly detailed, Gartner Magic Quadrant type graphs. They were weird. Remember, you choose the lens you want to look through. The type of information you require will all come down to how much detail you need to trust that the work is being done the way you want it. The ultimate reporting question is, "What do you need to know?"

There are two factors that help you get clear on what you need to know from an employee. The first thing to consider is information. Specifically, what is the *minimum* amount of information you need to keep you away from your email in the evenings? I call this the sleep factor. You do not want to be tossing in the middle of the night wondering if something did or did not get done. Your employee, selfishly, does not want this either. Focus on what is essential—what you need to know versus what you want to know.

Reporting is meant to build trust and show respect. You show respect to an employee by not asking for more information than you need. Choose your lens, and then leave the focus where you have set it.

In a sense, daily details are no longer any of your business. Daily details are not your job or your problem, so they aren't of any value to you. What you should know are the key three-to-five things that move the needle for this person's role. Once you have zeroed in on those needle-moving details, you have all you need to know about the inner workings of the employee's work. Just be sure these reporting metrics tie back to the employee's tasks.

METRICS, METRICS, METRICS

Now that we have established a structure for reporting, let's talk about metrics, which are the insights you will gain from your various reporting meetings. If you want to create your own metrics, broadly speaking, there are two types to consider. The two types are *quantity* and *competency*.

We will discuss a high-level overview of both in a second. But while we are talking about metrics, it is important to note that most industries already have established metrics for all sorts of roles. It is in your best interest to seek those out, decide which ones matter to you, and slot them into your reporting system with a frequency that makes the most sense to your business. If you cannot find ones that fit your business, use the overview below to build your own.

QUANTITY

Quantity-based metrics are concerned with output and the goals of output. If an employee works within a project, you want to know how they are meaningfully progressing in that project. This could look like them reporting on the number of milestones achieved or the number of items built within a certain time frame. If the work they do is turnkey or leans toward maintenance-oriented work, your metrics should be married to the time-blocking methods of PEB, QtC, or industry standardization.

Quantity-based metrics are concerned with throughput. A few examples are as follows. For a lawncare service, throughput is the number of yards mowed per day. For a salon, it's the number of haircuts per stylist, per day. For a used car dealership, it might be the number of five-year-old sedans sold per weekend.

This type of metric does not have to be so direct. If a role has task themes that have dependent responsibilities, such as lawn care personnel who also upsell landscaping, you can link them together. For instance, let's say we want our lawncare technicians to attempt an upsell of new flower beds whenever they finish mowing a yard. In this example, you could report on their upsells by linking the number of lawns mowed to the number of flowerbed opportunities that were converted. You then get a fuller picture of "mowing job quality," the opportunity cost for flower beds, as well as better indicators of business health.

Quantity-based metrics tell you whether the business is getting enough energy to meet the demands of the consumer.

COMPETENCY

Unlike quantity, competency-based metrics are notoriously difficult to define. But they are still important. Roles that demand soft skills, such as ones in HR, marketing, and sales may have competency-driven metrics. Examples of competency-driven metrics are how many impressions an ad campaign received or the outcomes gathered from a meeting with disgruntled clients. Build out these types of metrics for the purpose of understanding how an employee is favorably maintaining or growing the business.

With competency-based metrics, your primary concern is what an employee learned after a project or situation has transpired. You are not necessarily looking for only positive outcomes. You are, however, looking for an honest read on the knowledge they have acquired since you last met.

You calibrate competency with good questions. So reporting, for employees who primarily lean on their soft skills or qualitative work, should be focused on a series of qualifying questions about their work. The questions you ask an employee help you understand trends in the way the person works, thereby helping you evaluate their performance. Okay, enough theory. Here is how this might look in the wild. Let's say you have hired a marketer and have decided to let them handle all of your social media marketing. No more Facebook Reels for you. Hurray.

Let's say you also decided that brand awareness is what you want to measure. You cannot directly tie brand awareness to sales, at least not yet, but it is still an important factor if you hope to compete with larger companies in the future. How do you tell whether your marketer is performing well when it comes to owning brand awareness?

You will gauge performance based on a set of questions you ask in each reporting meeting. Using our previous example for reference, here are some questions you might ask:

- What was the sentiment from commenters on posts?
- How many people saw this campaign versus the last one?
- Has anyone from sales mentioned whether customers saw the campaign?

- What goals did you have for the campaign, and do you feel like you have met them?

- How have you contrasted our brand voice from our competition?

There is basically one takeaway from these types of questions: you want to get a read on how someone perceives the reality of work they are doing. For instance, if you spoke with an HR rep about how they handled the termination process for contractors, you would ask questions that got to the root of how they felt the conversations went, what the contractors said, and how the contractors' projects were closed out. You use this "sentiment" derived knowledge to build a basis for understanding how well an employee perceives the work they do. You then use this knowledge to identify patterns in performance, whether good or bad.

NO OFFENSE

Finally, do not put an employee on the defensive by reporting metrics. Reporting is not about defending decisions. Reporting is about understanding progress toward a goal. There will, of course, be situations where an employee must defend the numbers or the reasoning in their decisions, but their defense should be the exception and not the rule.

I have seen managers who like a good fight or challenge and think of reporting as a way to exercise their umpire skills. This type of energy is best saved for peers, or better yet, a CrossFit membership. An employee who is constantly playing defense will cause needless friction in your business. Reporting is meant to be a structured time to build trust, communicate metrics, and celebrate success.

I was once in a situation like this where I was required to report on the financial performance of the business, even though my role was not tied directly to revenue. Once a month, I had to defend profits and losses even though I had no influence over the numbers. The reporting requirement was frustrating because I had no control over sales, pricing, or new offerings. I could offer no detail other than conjecture when I gave a report. Every time I reported on sales, I had to first go get the number and then do a defensive dance with management about why the numbers were low. The lesson here is simple: only require an employee to report on a metric when they can control the outcome. If you do require them to report on a metric that is indirectly correlated with their role, be sure to teach them how it is connected to their work.

Facts focus the conversation when the time comes to give a report. Without these grounding details, your meetings with an employee will be vague, and you will never know the true performance of their role. Wherever you lack clarity, there will also be a lack of trust and a lack of information to help you operate the business with excellence. But once you have your facts straight, you can move on to forecasting.

ON FORECASTING

The final factor of good reporting is concerned with future performance. A healthy business is mechanical, but people are not machines. For a business to grow in increasing efficiency, people and their work need to be continually calibrated to work at their best. In order for this to happen, you need to look at historical performance to predict future outcomes.

FORECASTING VERSUS GUT INSTINCT

Entrepreneurs need to incorporate good forecasting to stay away from guessing games, such as relying on gut instinct to make decisions. Gut instinct is great for making decisions in the moment, but your gut is not prophetic. Good forecasting, on the other hand, can tell you how to plan and what business outcomes may be in the future based on what you know today.

Forecasting is also useful for understanding where an employee's role is headed, whether they are ahead or behind in their work. With good planning, you can use forecasting to predict whether your business is on track to meet larger goals or whether it may be falling short of the opportunities you see in front of you. With metrics, the foundation is trust, while with forecasting, the foundation is trends. Trends in data tell you whether the employee is on or off track to meet the goals of their role and the business.

In this sense, forecasting is simple. Forecasting answers the question, "Are we on track or off track?" A little deviation from a trend is fine—like a stock price, the day-in-day-out details may show fluctuations toward a larger goal. The overall trend should be toward an increase in performance until the upper-limit thresholds of performance are met.

When these upper limits are met, it is time to promote an employee, multiply their role, or change expectations about what your business is capable of producing. These are nice problems to have—but you should not have to worry about them for a while.

HOW TO FORECAST PERFORMANCE

To get started with forecasting, you simply need to compare the metrics of a role against larger business goals. Let's say you hire someone to make sales calls for you with the goal of increasing sales from $500,000 a year to $1,000,000 a year. For the sake of simplicity, let's say you know they need to make 50 phone calls a day, with the assumption that they will successfully close 25 percent of those sales calls, in order to meet your end-of-year sales goal. In this scenario, you have your benchmark goal (50 phone calls a day), and the salesperson's performance (say 37 calls a day). Some days, they may exceed their goal; other days, they may fall short. So, you need to see the gap between their performance and the goal get smaller so that the business can grow as you intend. But these numbers alone are not enough. You also need to look at how meaningful the numbers are to employee performance.

LEADING AND LAGGING PERFORMANCE

As with tasks, forecasting is also concerned with performance. The difference here is that we are predicting performance versus measuring performance. In forecasting, performance insights are also a combination of *leading* and *lagging* indicators. Leading and lagging indicators are used in all sorts of business development frameworks like OKRS, KPIs, and specialized measures like NPS, but the concept is simple, and you can use them in your business too.

Leading indicators tell you if something looks as if performance is going according to plan. In our example, this would be the number of phone calls. If someone makes 45–55 calls a day, this should indicate that they will meet their sales goal and the new revenue goal for the company. This number, however, will inevitably only tell half the story. You will also need lagging indicators to tell you whether or not those numbers are making an impact in the business.

A sales executive I knew hired a salesperson with a lot of promise, but their experience highlights the need for both types of performance indicators. Out of the gate, the salesperson exceeded their goal of 100 phone calls a day. The employee was praised in meetings, earned employee of the month, and quickly became popular with their boss. Despite this, they were let go within the same year they were hired.

The reason they were let go was because they were not good at closing any sales calls. On the surface, they were charismatic, proactive, and quick to call all their leads—meeting their call quota regularly. But they were not a good salesperson because they were actually very bad at closing. This is what we mean by a lagging indicator.

Lagging indicators tell you whether the initial numbers are good or bad. The lagging indicator, in this case, would be the close rate as a ratio to the number of calls being made. In this scenario, around 13 percent of sales calls should have resulted in a sale, but the salesperson's close rate was actually much lower. Other team members on the sales team had much lower call counts, as low as 75 calls a day, but their closing ratio was much higher, resulting in more revenue for the company.

Both numbers, the number of calls and the number of closed sales, told the executive whether the performance was actually leading to a good revenue trend for the business. Without both numbers, their forecasting would have gaps. Moreover, it would be hard to discern what was causing the dip in revenue projections.

In this situation, the manager might have been tempted to think only the close rate was important since this told them the actual sales and revenue increase of the business. But without the number of calls, they would not know if the money spent on salary for the salesperson was causing a loss for the business.

When you combine leading and lagging indicators, you can create benchmarks for the performance of your employee. In this way, you can plot out, over time, whether or not a person is successful in their role and use that performance to forecast the future of your business.

BENCHMARKING

Once you have decided on how and when you want reports to be held, you can then start to benchmark performance. Over time, benchmarking allows you to create a template for what performance should look like for new employees. As an example, you may start with the assumption that a new salesperson could increase revenue by 50 percent, but historical performance may tell you that in reality, a good salesperson can, at best, only increase revenue by 27 percent over an eighteen-month period. Without this data, you may assume that an employee is underperforming when in reality, it is your assumption that is over-expectant of what can be produced.

Herein lies the benefit of forecasting. Forecasting makes you a more sophisticated and empathic manager. This, in turn, makes you a better business leader and someone who is more trusted by both your employees and peers—all of which leads to higher retention rates and better performance of the business.

When you master the principles of the third floor, you become a sophisticated manager. Sophisticated managers know that it is not a hardline personality, overly ambitious goals, or pushing people past their limits that make a business successful. This is like pushing a high-performance vehicle past its oil change, with poor-quality gas, on a bumpy road, while trying to win a race. The car may be up for the challenge, but it will eventually break down. Good drivers, however, are aware of the vehicle's limits and where it performs best. They know that the right inputs create the right outputs in performance. They also take it on themselves to know how to make the vehicle drive at peak performance.

When you design good rhythms of reporting and you know the clear indicators of performance, you will be a true entrepreneurial manager. I say true manager because you will be managing from reality, from numbers and facts, and not your gut or instincts—both of which will make you anxious when not anchored in real data.

Employees thrive when you trust the data surrounding their role. In this trust-cultivated culture, it will only be a matter of time before they outgrow their current role and continue to grow the business. Herein lies your access to the fourth floor—your greatest point of leverage.

CHAPTER 11

SHOW WHAT YOU DO: THE FOURTH FLOOR

KURT WAS A TALENTED CONTRIBUTOR turned regional manager. He came up through the ranks of a nonprofit with the steady progress of a standout leader. His diligence served him well. Before long, he was picking new people for his team, and everyone he hired performed well under his guidance.

Kurt's boss, however, had a different reputation. If someone performed poorly, they were branded incapable of learning. If a person made a mistake, the upper manager immediately started micromanaging them, referencing articles they read about how the person should do their work. Worse, they would often try to do the work themselves to prove they knew more than the person who did the job.

Full of distrust, the big boss would label people as either having talent or not having talent, having work ethic or not having work ethic—basically they either had *it* or they did not. There was little in between. Their behavior stood in stark contrast to Kurt's approach to growing and promoting people.

Kurt used an approach to promotion that he dubbed "patterns." A person's patterns told Kurt whether an employee was trustworthy or not in their work. Patterns also told him whether they could handle more responsibility without his direct guidance. His approach to patterns, like management, was simple.

To establish a pattern, he would give a team member a specific task that was easy to manage and was in line with the type of work he thought they would enjoy. Once the person completed their task, he reviewed their work, performed a retrospective meeting of some kind, and then either kept the employee on the task, paired them with a team member for support, or gave them more responsibility in the future. Kurt would repeat the process again until he saw a pattern of behavior emerge. The process was simple, but because of his approach, his team members grew to trust him almost as quickly as they were promoted within their team.

Kurt was also quick to let individuals live up to their potential. You might say this was good leadership and of course, you would be right. But the approach also let Kurt scale his efforts quicker than other managers within the organization.

You see, Kurt did not waste time learning new skills to be the most competent person on his team. In truth, most of his team members were more highly skilled than him. He did understand their work, and sometimes he would model their work at the onset of training, but he was always quick to let people take over once he saw a pattern of behavior that told him they could be trusted.

You might think the kudos he received were rewarding enough, but Kurt gained something else as well. Kurt had all the time he needed to expand his business partnerships—something that was of utmost importance to him. Without realizing it, Kurt had gained access to the fourth floor: *Show what you do.*

The fourth and final floor is Show What You Do. Simply put, this floor operates on the principle that there is someone on your team who both *knows* more and can *do* more than you in a particular area of your business. The fourth floor is the most desirable one because it shifts the most work away from you.

You see, the first three floors were about addition. You added talent, you added time, and you added clarity to your business. Each time you and your employee went up a floor, the new perspective gave you a little more time and a little more access to better results within your business. However, where the first three floors only added benefit to your business—on the fourth floor, you will multiply your efforts and the benefit you receive from a higher perspective. It is here, on the fourth floor, that you get the most leverage of your time because you have the least amount of oversight.

THE FOURTH FLOOR PARADOX

For some entrepreneurs, the fourth floor feels like a paradox because you get more done with next-to-no effort—something unheard of if you are used to relying on your effort and talent to get things done. The reason? The employee can see just as far, if not farther, than you.

The fourth floor completely removes you from the work equation and gives the power of delegation to the original person to whom you first delegated work. Now, you are not just a manager of people, but you empower them as well.

The fourth floor is special because it also passes the torch of delegation. The fourth floor acknowledges the ultimate expertise of the individual you hired and uses that expertise to completely remove you from the process of owning outcomes.

The fourth floor may feel unnerving, but the natural progression of good delegation, coupled with a good employee, is that the person doing the work will grow in their capacity to make your business even more successful.

In our earlier example, many of Kurt's team members went on to lead teams of their own, sometimes with more direct reports than him, often in less than a year. In large part, this had to do with the way he helped them leverage their own expertise on their path to management.

This leads us to an important consideration for those you choose to hire: you should never hire someone whom you cannot see promoting in the future. Moreover, you should never create a role for work that you are not willing to let have a life of its own. If you create a halfhearted role, you will break the managerial machine.

WHAT THEY SHOULD DO NEXT

Just as a child who hits a growth spurt will need new clothes, an employee will need to put on new responsibilities as they continue to do what they do best. Eventually, they will outgrow the responsibilities they were originally hired to do. When they trigger this tipping point you have three options:

You can let them go. If you choose this option, you choose to maintain your business's present market share. You let them go because the business has grown more than you secretly desire.

You can deepen their role. If you choose this option, you want the individual's expertise to make your brand more widely recognized for a certain type of discipline or skill.

You can make them a manager. If you choose this option, you want the individual to continue growing the business, and you are willing to let the principles of The Elevator Effect repeat itself in the work life of the individual you are about to promote.

Let's look at each option in more detail.

OPTION ONE: LET THEM GO

The first option is to fire them. You might think this is a little tongue in cheek, but it is not. If you do not want your business to grow, and you only want to maintain what you have built thus far, then you need to clue the employee into this revelation and give them a gracious runway for success somewhere else. You should not, however, hold them back with false promises of future promotion or greater ownership. Be honest with yourself about what your business is, and you will have more peace about who you are as an entrepreneurial manager as well.

I have known business leaders who talked of being world-class and taking on all the competition, only to intentionally keep their business from growing by not taking on new accounts or even intentionally throttling their own growth. They were not world-class. They were best-in-class or best-in-region. Not that there is anything wrong with that accomplishment. If you know your market category well enough, then you should also know when your business hits its upper limits as well.

A C-level manager I knew always described their business as if it were a unicorn with billion-dollar potential. In reality, their business was the same size as twenty-two other similar companies. Not to mention, their operational constraints prevented them from getting much larger.

Again, there is nothing wrong with this reality, but it is, in fact, reality. The reason I belabor this point is that your employees should also have a clear understanding of where your business, and their role within it, are headed. This helps the employee apply their time in the best way possible. Many a disgruntled employee will leave a business after giving their all to it—when giving their all was not necessary. Giving what was *needed* was necessary.

It goes without saying that knowing what work is necessary to the business is up to you, the manager, to communicate and decide upon. If you only intend to grow a business's efficiency and not its revenue, then reverse engineer that into the role of the employee. If you do want to grow the business in all respects, you have two more options at your disposal.

OPTION TWO: DEEPEN THE ROLE

A colleague of mine, whom we will call Bob, could do it all. He was a proverbial jack of all trades—and his boss knew it. Bob's main talent was in human resources, but Bob's boss had him trade his time for administrative work, number-crunching, and even going to the grocery store to pick up snacks when he had nothing else to do. Bob could do all these things and more, but Bob got frustrated with the constant context switching. Furthermore, since Bob traded his time for a range of menial tasks, he had nothing in the way of reputation.

Because Bob was not a focused employee, he offered no real value to the business. This was not obvious to his boss, who suffered from the junk-drawer mentality, but it did have an effect on Bob. For good reason, he eventually left the company.

The truth is, Bob was a very caring person who understood people. He used to be a leader at his church, and he knew how to help alleviate the daily stresses of other people. He also wanted to help the business perform to its utmost potential.

Had his boss recognized this skill, he could have grown Bob's role in the direction of HR and given him deeper, more meaningful work while also supporting the business's growing team.

Since Bob was so caring and wanted to please his manager, he would gladly take on any work in an attempt to make himself more useful. But his obligatory tendencies actually made him less useful because he was so scattered. It is important to note that Bob did not want to manage people, either. Deeping his role, instead of widening it, would have been a better solution.

DEEPEN THE ROLE INSTEAD OF MAKING IT WIDER

Many managers, especially those in smaller businesses, will widen the responsibilities of an employee—giving them work outside their main line of responsibility. This looks like giving an accountant the job of cleaning up Excel documents because you think they are good with numbers, or giving a baker work as a confectioner because both types of work happen over a stove. In general, making someone a generalist makes them feel less valuable. It also reduces their throughput by making them less focused.

You have probably met a doctor who was irked at being asked for medical advice outside their field of expertise. The same is true in your business. A professional does not a profession make. Managers who over-assign work typically do so in an effort to recover more time without letting go of too much profit. In a pinch, this feels like a good decision. It is a costly mistake.

An employee who has a role that is constantly widened will get frustrated with their lack of focus and eventually leave. This leaves the manager in a worse position than before the role was created. The solution is to deepen the role. The only exception is if the role is designed to be multi-disciplined in nature.

Deepening a role builds on the employee's expertise by making them leaders within their existing domain of responsibility. This reinforcement of their role, in turn, gives clout to your business. If the employee is a leader, then so, in turn, is your business. Deeping the role has the added benefit of fulfilling the employee's need for meaningful growth and connection to their work as well.

If you choose to deepen an employee's role, you are also choosing to let go of any more expertise you have in that area. This is the power of the fourth floor.

They now know more and can do more than you previously could if you had their role.

This makes you an expert in management and them an expert in their field. The lines of management are now as clearly separate as they can be—they manage decisions and you manage time.

Here, one of the great manifestations of the fourth floor appears. When a role is deepened, you let the employee manage decisions. You still manage the role, but the decisions within that role fall firmly on the hire. The hire can even go as far as to make decisions without your input because your input—at least in this part of the business—is now less important or helpful than it was before. Yes, this will require new reporting metrics on your part, but reports are meant to grow with a role anyway.

THE RIGHT TIME TO DEEPEN A ROLE

At this point, the question that falls on many managers' minds is *when* to let an employee make those all-important business-building decisions for themselves? The answer to this question lies in the employee's previous performance, i.e., their patterns.

A person's behavioral patterns tell you whether they will do well in other parts of your business. If they are faithful in small things, they will be faithful in greater responsibilities. However, it is not just their responsibility and excellence that you should be concerned about. You also want to know that the way in which they work will work in other areas of the business too.

If an employee is creative and good at problem-solving, they will not give up those ways of thinking in a new role. The same is true if they are analytical and process-driven. Those ways of working will see greater potential if their role is deepened and given more responsibility. The all-important question is whether they are ready to move into that role, with those behaviors, when the time comes for the decision to be made. You need to help the employee with that decision.

An employee may desire to have more responsibility before they are ready to handle it. If this is the case, then you need to set clear expectations about when they will be ready to make that shift to business-building decisions. This shift could occur when certain milestones are met or when the business hits certain revenue marks to which they have contributed. Regardless of the evidence, the employee should be able to meet that expectation of their own fruition. Now, if they have already met those expectations, then it is time to let them make decisions for themselves.

Lastly, be honest with yourself. You may not feel ready for this transition. If the shift in responsibility makes you uncomfortable, go back to the third floor and decide what data will support your ability to trust them more fully in the new role. If you are up for it, let the employee decide what those data points should be. They are, after all, the expert.

OPTION THREE: MAKE THEM A MANAGER

The third option available to you is to make the person a manager of a team for which they were previously a direct contributor. If they have demonstrated their ability to make good decisions and contribute to growth, then they may be ready to start building a team themselves. Now, they will take their own team up the elevator.

If you choose to make an employee a manager, your role with them will become one of both manager and mentor. You will continue to manage them, but they are now the expert in implementation. So, moving forward in this decision, you set the expectations for what will make them a good manager.

In this phase of their professional growth, you begin again with the first and second floors of delegation—you help them get into the managerial mindset, shifting them from *doing* work to *managing* work. You also set up a process to help them transfer what they know to a new hire and set expectations for what the new role (or roles) underneath them will do.

If you choose option three, there are a couple of risks to bear in mind. First, you need to know if they can manage effectively. Second, you need to help them decide who their first team member will be.

ABILITY TO MANAGE EFFECTIVELY

With this risk, you are evaluating whether they can manage their time effectively and also step away from the work they used to do. You want to know if they have a mind for processes and a propensity for championing the vision of their department—not to mention, the business at large.

Before this individual steps into management, you need to discern whether new hires would thrive in a team where they might report to this person. You discover this by observing how they pay attention to manager-level details. A good manager knows why the details are important and not just how to execute the details effectively.

This does not mean they need to be a through-and-through leader with the communication skills of Tony Robbins. That role belongs to you. They should, however, be able to mentally zoom in and out, gracefully guiding an individual through the *why* and the *how* of daily responsibilities—navigating them to outcomes and not just outputs.

If you are unsure of whether they have the innate ability to manage, then trial them in the role. You can test their abilities by letting them manage simple tasks with someone such as an intern. In this scenario, you will test their managerial potential with low-risk but heavily process-oriented tasks. You take this approach to see how they communicate and follow up with tasks that have a low impact on the business. If they fail, there is little fallout and you have learned something new.

If you choose to test their managerial ability, I recommend that you do not let them know they are being tested. Just communicate that you want them to manage the *why* and *how* of a small project. Once your manager-in-training feels the test project is complete, host an informal meeting so they can debrief you on how it went.

In the meeting, pay attention to how they communicate about the person's performance and not just the project's completion. Did they notice how the person they managed thought about the work? Did they notice where each of them struggled and why? Were they able to communicate why the project benefited the larger organism of the team? Most importantly, were they able to separate the person's performance from their value as an individual? These cues clue you into whether they have a talent for management. Again, we are not looking for expert-level management, we are looking for their potential for management.

Lastly, pay attention to whether they enjoyed this little trial or whether they seemed to gravitate right back to wanting to do their own job. Unless they are extremely busy in their own role, there should be a level of satisfaction in seeing someone else be successful. This satisfaction is the ultimate litmus test of whether they will be successful in a managerial role.

THEIR FIRST TEAM MEMBER

The second risk is all about succession. Here, the employee may need help deciding which part of their previous work to offload first. Unless you have a lot of employees with similar expertise, then there is a good chance this new manager will not offload all of their responsibilities in one major transition. Moreover, you also do not want to widen another employee's role just because this person has outgrown their own.

The key to a successful transition is to look at the employee's "day in a life." We are not talking about the Beatles here. An employee's "day in a life" is a breakdown of the work they do. Some work may need to continue temporarily as they transition. Other bits can probably be offloaded more quickly. You decide what can be offloaded based on risk to the business and key responsibilities that need to be done.

As an example, let's say you own a restaurant, and your employee is responsible for helping people check out. But they also help with food prep in between assisting purchase decisions. The plan is to transition them into a new role where they train new hires to perform line work. Because the checkout process is high-touch, people-focused, and affects your brand, you may need to keep them in this part of their role while their new team member takes over food prep—a more process-oriented and easily trainable set of tasks. The new team member may take over the checkout counter as well, but only after shadowing your new manager for an appropriate amount of time, following their onboarding.

Let's look at another example for a creative agency. If you are in a project-based business, such as a creative agency, you may keep the employee on an existing creative project that is still in play, while also moving them to manage a new project that just began. They will still handle creative decisions on the previous project, but they will start the new project on the basis of client management rather than direct contribution. The way to prioritize these types of decisions is by determining what is mission critical to the role and what is not.

You can also plan a transition based purely on what is process-driven and therefore easy to train, in contrast with work that requires more soft skills or a more nuanced understanding of your business—things that will take time for a new hire to learn and appreciate. Either way, set up some time with your manager-to-be and create a plan to offload tasks that are considered low risk. Let them continue the critical tasks. Just be sure to communicate and decide when the remainder of those responsibilities will also move to someone else. This way, the new manager can continue to focus on gaining the benefits of The Elevator Effect.

WRAPPING UP

Of course, with all three promotion options, consult with the employee directly. Get their feedback and perspective about the decision you must make. Also, do not choose option one or two for them. Not every employee wants to move into management. That is okay. Their input may lead you to hire a new manager or expand the functions of the team to compensate for their decision.

When the time comes to make a decision about their role, set up a meeting with the employee. In the meeting, frame the conversation around their positive performance. As you go through their performance, reference specific metrics and commitments in which they have excelled. As you continue to frame the conversation around their previous successes, lead them to the crossroads you have in front of you. The business is growing, and they are the reason for the growth. Tell them you want them to continue to contribute to that growth but also want their input with how the growth continues.

How would they feel about leading a team? Would they prefer more responsibility in their existing type of work? These types of questions help the employee feel in control of their work life. You will also benefit from their honest feedback about the future of your business.

The benefits of the fourth floor are wonderful. At this level, you get the highest potential access to your time and more fulfillment in your entrepreneurial career. You have now multiplied your time and your effectiveness.

Now that you have access to the fourth floor, you graduate from simply being an entrepreneurial manager-in-training to being a mentor as well. You are no longer simply an operator but a leader too—an incredible achievement on your part. To continue benefiting from this achievement, you need to motivate your staff for the long haul, not just the short sprints of a hiring frenzy. You will do this with some advanced managerial strategies.

CHAPTER 12

HOW TO PRIORITIZE WHAT YOU DELEGATE NEXT

AS AN ENTREPRENEUR, BOTH YOU and your business are on a transformational journey. This journey begins with a destination and is realized through delivery toward that destination. This journey starts with you in the driver's seat.

Just like a road trip across the United States, your business journey will have several pitstops and milestones along the way. As you pass them, you also pass off more and more delivery work. At first, you were the only person who drove. But now, that will change. From here on out, what you do with your time depends on where you are headed.

Your job, as an entrepreneur, is to regularly evaluate this road trip, the milestones you are achieving, and the work you are doing. Every time you hit a significant milestone, some of your old work stays and some of it goes. Your business intuition knows this already.

You probably have a gut sense when you are doing the *wrong* kind of work. But when you have been driving for a long time, it is hard to self-evaluate your performance. Are you going too fast? Should you have stopped for gas earlier on? Should you go somewhere other than where you are presently headed? When you do nothing but drive, it is hard to tell. This is why some entrepreneurs get stuck in stagnant companies for years. They cannot take their foot off the gas pedal for fear the bridge is out. Here's the kicker, intuition alone will not tell you what you need to do next.

You get your work in the right order by getting clear on the upcoming milestones of your business, and then aligning that with your role as a business leader. Said another way, you need to distinguish between the ultimate destination of your business and your progress toward its next milestone. Milestones bring clarity to management. You do not want to prematurely delegate work, but you also do not want to wait too long.

ONE ROAD, THREE MILESTONES

There are three main types of milestones. They include revenue, operational excellence, and brand development. These milestones are not in any particular order, however, you will pass all of them in your destination toward a stable and thriving business. Your next milestone depends on the relative maturity of your business. The all-important question is—what should you be doing so that someone else can do the work of driving toward that next important milestone for you?

As we discussed earlier, our decisions are driven by our values and our values guide us to ever-higher uses of our time. With this in mind, we have to prioritize our work—shifting work to its appropriate categories. If you put work in the wrong category, it throttles your business performance.

THE FOUR LEVELS OF PRIORITY

You move toward your next important milestone by deciding which work you keep, and which work you delegate. You get this clarity as a business leader by putting work into four different levels of priority. Let's quickly look at a summary of each one.

IMMEDIATE DELEGATION

Immediate delegation is for time-consuming, low-value work. This work prevents you from growing your business and owning the vision required of you. *Beware.* The definition of "low value" changes as you pass certain milestones.

EVENTUAL DELEGATION

Eventual delegation is for work that currently *only* you can do but *could* be learned by someone else. For now, it is on you, but you need to get it off your plate as soon as responsibly possible.

ESCALATED DELEGATION

Escalated delegation is reserved for scenarios where you should own the work but cannot because of some unforeseen constraint. You only delegate this type of work in an emergency or where time is of the essence. You also only give this work to someone who grasps its impact and has some history with the work already.

NEVER DELEGATED

Work you never delegate is any work that drives your business mission, is visionary, and focuses on future milestones. You free up your time so you can put more focus on this work.

UNPACKING THE FOUR PRIORITIZATION LEVELS

The four levels serve the *why* of entrepreneurial management. They tell you why you do or do not focus on certain aspects of your business. To this end, the four levels act as a kind of offloading tool to help you delegate all work that does not serve the highest use of your time. Use them as a sliding scale for making good decisions about the work ahead—both the things you need to do now, and the things that come in the natural course of running your business. As you will see, you will use each prioritization level to influence how you build out a delegation plan using The Triad method you learned earlier in the book.

LOW VALUE, HIGH VALUE, LITTLE TO NO VALUE

Reference the visualization on the following page as you start to consider what you should delegate next. As you can see, the different categories of work demand varying levels of time from you. But they also give you varying levels of value as well. Work you need to delegate immediately takes a lot of your time but provides very little value to the milestones you want to achieve. Conversely, work that needs an escalation plan should not require any of your time but will give you a lot of value when a plan is in place.

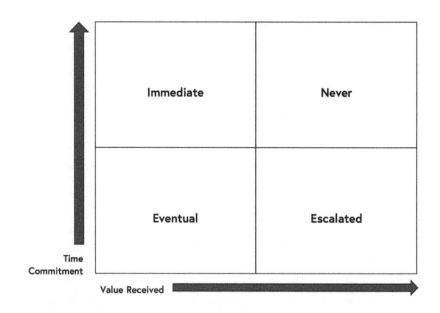

Download The Free Template!

Get the **Delegation Matrix** template along with other great tools included with this book at:

https://piercebrantley.co/NYJ-downloads

Now let's look at each prioritization level a little closer to determine how you might get the most from what they offer.

TASKS TO DELEGATE IMMEDIATELY

We have all heard stories of the self-sacrificing CEO who swept floors or washed windows in an effort to show servant leadership or an extreme commitment to humility. These stories make for a great episode of Undercover Boss or an inspirational LinkedIn post, but they do not make for good management. An entrepreneurial manager who spends all their time doing work that maintains the business will soon have a business that is unmaintainable and unmanageable. So low-value work is work that needs to be done but is not strategic to running the business or growing revenue. We seek to delegate low-value work immediately.

We do not frame low-value work as demeaning or punitive work—low-value work has value. Someone will do it, and they need to continue to do it well—it just will not be you.

For instance, if the owner of a bakery cleans the floors of the shop every thirty minutes, it will make the store more inviting, but it will also detract from researching the best products to sell. Similarly, the owner of a design agency may know how to create a beautiful letterhead or presentation template for clients, but it detracts from the work of securing new business. Low-value work is work that you are capable of doing but detracts from the highest use of your time.

TIME AUDITS

Use time audits to discover where you spend your time. Perhaps you already know what you need to stop doing, but if you need ideas, you can use a tool I like to call a *time audit*. A time audit tells you precisely where you spend your time and the value you get from your daily work.

The time audit is simple. To start, record everything you do for a week. Do not change anything about how you work or the speed at which you get things done. Just record everything you do in the order that you do it. At the end of the week, organize all the work you did into categorical levels of importance.

The levels of importance include *mission-critical*, *important*, and *low-value* work. You keep mission-critical work. Mission-critical work will not be delegated. Important work is shortlisted for *eventual* or *escalated delegation*. Low-value work should be removed from your calendar immediately. Here is an example of a business owner's Wednesday:

Wednesday		Time Audit
Task	Time Spent	Importance
Business Partnership Mtg.	2 hours	Mission Critical
Brand Strategy Session w/ Agency	1.5 hours	Mission Critical
Continue Research of West Coast Competition	2 hours	Important
Wash Company Vehicle	30 minutes	Low Value
Interview w/ Local Magazine	30 minutes	Mission Critical
Update Website with New Product Offering	30 minutes	Important
Restock Snack Fridge	45 minutes	Low Value
Update Client on Project Process	1 Hour	Important
Quick Lead Qualification Meeting	15 minutes	Important
Go to Job Site and See Contractor Progress	1 hour	Important
Time Spent	**10 hours**	
Mission-Critical Work	4 hours	
Other Work	6 hours	
Percent Of Reclaimable Time	**60 percent**	

Download The Free Template!

Get the **Time Audit** template along with other great tools included with this book at:

https://piercebrantley.co/NYJ-downloads

As you can see in our example, in one day alone, sixty percent of this business owner's day was spent on work that was not critical to the role of building their business. Imagine all the lost opportunity, and the cost of losing that opportunity, simply because they were not actively tracking where their time was spent. Over the course of the year, this could result in millions of dollars' worth of unrealized profit. Not to mention the devaluing of the owner's salary and role. This is why the time audit is so useful.

After you conduct your own audit, review your week in detail, categorizing all the work you did. Once you know how your time is spent, make a plan to quickly remove *low-value* work. Aim to do so in a month's time, sooner if possible. Low-value work keeps you busy but unproductive. Aim to get an intern, virtual assistant, or third-party service to tackle this category for you.

For all your work in the *important* category, go back to The Triad methodology and create a reasonable plan to bring on someone new who you can train to do the work for you. You will find this work often falls into work you can delegate *eventually*.

Continue to periodically conduct a time audit whenever you push past a significant shift or milestone in your business's growth. You will always find new things that creep onto your calendar which no longer belong.

WORK YOU NEED TO DELEGATE EVENTUALLY

Some work needs a roadmap to be offloaded responsibly. This type of work requires a higher level of skill and is normally critical to the value your business produces. So it needs a succession plan of sorts. Here, you need to create a plan to prevent your business from lurching to a stop if you were to quit it tomorrow.

I had a situation like this as a Product Owner for a tech company. In this role, I determined what we would build, who would use it, and all the important details that went into how the work got done. The work was high-value, but I had to move into managing long-term goals, not the projects themselves.

My team needed a solution that slowly gave this product work to someone else—all without our steady delivery coming to a halt. We made a plan. In short, we offloaded the work, project by project, to a new person, until it naturally fell off my plate. The entire transition process went smoothly because we created task themes using the process from the first portion of The Triad. From there, I managed that person like I would anyone else. I never had to pick up the projects again, except when they related to product vision.

Use theme-based succession plans like this for work that is high-value but also highly time intensive for you. The critical factor for deciding whether to get rid of this type of work lies in whether it is strategic to business development or owns vision in some way. If it is not, then create a deadline to find the right person to succeed you. Always remember that the temptation with this type of work is to continue doing it, in part, because you enjoy it or are good at getting it done. This is why I recommend you set a deadline.

WORK YOU NEED TO ESCALATE TO SOMEONE ELSE

As a business owner, you also need to plan for contingencies—times when things do not go according to plan. When the business is just you, or you are the only person held responsible for emergencies, you are not likely to plan for emergencies because you are both the fire station and firefighter. You run the ladder and put out fires as they come. But when your team grows, this will not always be possible. It makes sense to start building out a plan for how you will handle things when you are away from the business.

A senior manager I knew ran into an escalation scenario and it highlights why they can be so hampering to an entrepreneur's time. The situation happened while they were on vacation. Well, almost on vacation. They ran a SaaS business but did not have a plan for online outages.

An outage occurred the same day they left for some much needed R&R. No one in the business had the skills to bring the business back online. Sadly, they had to cancel their plans just hours after their plane landed in vacationland. Call me crazy, but escalations always seem to happen when a vacation is scheduled. Had this person created a plan for outages, and designated point-people for this type of emergency, their plan would have carried the weight for resolving the issue—instead of them.

For this type of work, you need to identify where your business could have *potential* operational risks. For instance, if cannot answer a client's important question, determine who *could* answer it in your absence. If your business relies on a supply chain running smoothly, determine where failures could happen and how they would be handled if you were not there to fix the issue.

Short-list these risks, and assign an escalation plan to someone who you know could solve the problem in a pinch. Communicate to this person that they are the owner of these problems when you are unavailable.

The goal is to make a business that has no problem with problems. Escalations are just one of many things it can handle without you.

WAR ROOM WORKSHOPS

If you want to ace escalations, I recommend you create a type of war room workshop where you create scenarios that highlight and quantify the types of risks associated with a potential escalation. In the workshop, you want to identify the exact nature of the risk, the scale of the risk, and to the extent possible, the effect it might have on your business. Most important, you need to identify a point person.

This designated point person will handle the scenario if you are not available. You might even want someone to handle the scenario if you *are* available, on principle. Even in an escalation, you do not want your time spent reacting to problems when it could be spent on mission-critical work. On the next page is an example of an escalation workshop output for a construction company.

Escalation Type	Risk Level
City Gas Line Broken	High

Scenario
City schematics for gas line pipework aren't always accurate, which can result in our team breaking an active gas line when laying foundations for new buildings. If this happens, we need to quickly control the situation to prevent extra costs to the project, sick employees, or worse, an explosion.

Quantifiable Risk
Loss of future projects with the city, valued at 13 million over the next two years. Potential injury of employees resulting in loss of staff and higher insurance premiums.

Point Person
Terrence Brooks, GM

Steps to Mitigate Risk	
Step One	Quickly turn off all power equipment.
Step Two	Clear the area to a minimum of 100 feet.
Step Three	Call the gas company and have them shut off the gas. If we have access to shut off the valve, then confirm closure.
Step Four	Collect documentation proving team called 811 and requested line marking prior to digging.

List of Important Contacts	
Mandy Newton Rep at Atmix Gas Corp	644–123–9500

Use an escalation template, like the one above, to create a series of playbooks that free you from high-risk, intensive work in your business. You will rest easy knowing that the right people have the right plan to handle even the most extreme of situations your business might encounter.

Download The Free Template!

Get the **Escalation Plan** template along with other great tools included with this book at:

https://piercebrantley.co/NYJ-downloads

WORK YOU WILL NEVER DELEGATE

Work you never delegate is work that is central to your business's strategy, vision, and growth. As a managerial figurehead, this type of work is driven by you. If you delegate this type of work, you delegate the soul of the business to someone else.

If your business is still in its early stages, then it may mean your transition is not purely vision focused but more of a quasi-operational role—one where you completely refocus on the next important phase of business-building, undistracted from the work you used to do. So long as this work is in alignment with the intended trajectory of your business, you are still working toward the right thing. You will not delegate this phase-based work until the business hits its next milestone of growth.

However, work you never intend to delegate is not siloed work. It does not live in a room on its own. For example, an entrepreneur who is an acting sales manager will absolutely get critical information from a sales analyst or a sales representative who helps them understand the pulse of sales in the business, but they would not delegate the decision of where to focus the team. This responsibility falls squarely on them. The things you choose to never delegate are all about ownership, not siloing information.

SUMMARY

Once you understand the four levels of handoff, you can confidently scale your role alongside that of your business. As your business grows, you will grow with it, and your old work will smoothly roll off to other people. Best of all, with prioritization in place, you gain an intuitive sense of what belongs on your plate now and what you can keep a little while longer.

After you have spent some time with the different levels, consider creating a plan for how you will hand off work as it aligns with the milestones you want to achieve in your business. If you have a solid long-term plan, you can even begin to craft roles and task themes ahead of time. This type of delegation plan will help you grow your business smoothly. If you do it right, it will help prevent you from getting bogged down in low-value work each time your business gets ready for its next stage of growth.

Now that you are a pro at prioritizing what you delegate, you can leverage two special methodologies of management that govern how people get their work done, not just what they do. If you use them right, you will have a business that is not just efficient but inspirational as well.

CHAPTER 13

TWO DELEGATION STRATEGIES AND HOW TO USE THEM

JUST LIKE A STARBUCKS double mocha Frappuccino, employees need a sweet blend of guidance and personal choice in order to feel like the work they do is worth the effort. Yes, they want to know how to perform their jobs well, but they do not want every decision to be vetted and scrutinized under a microscope. We call this desire autonomy, and in this way, employees have a sort of internal view of themselves as CEO, regarding their own, individual work.

Autonomy is a good thing if it has guardrails. As an entrepreneurial manager, you want to provide those guardrails so that people get as much done as possible without your direct supervision. To build these guardrails, you will implement two different kinds of delegation strategy. These two strategies serve as an underlying foundation for all the work and special assignments you divvy out.

PRINCIPLES AND PROCESSES

The two strategies are principle-driven delegation and process-driven delegation. Principles give employees agency to make decisions in difficult situations they cannot plan for. Processes give them a time-calibrated method to get work done in a methodical, predictable way.

All your newly acquired time will lean on these two planes of delegation. Just like a good foundation, they rest upon each other, giving the rest of your managerial decisions a predictable outcome. You need to combine both approaches to prevent your time from being stolen by things like customer escalations, project blockages, and the like. These types of problems will block you from making the best use of your time.

Do not react to problems. Plan for them.

We use the two methods because, without them, you are at the whim of any question a worker has for you. Help with a customer? They will ask you. Question about a project task? They will come to you. Someone's lunch break needs to shift an hour? They will expect you to help. While these types of questions might make you feel important, reactionary decision-making siphons away your time, and requires an employee to come to you for each and every gray area they encounter in their job. Reactionary decisions make you a reactionary manager and leader.

All this potential for reactionary decision-making defeats the purpose of hiring someone to begin with. You end up only managing questions and problems, making you a Senior Decision Manager, not an entrepreneurial manager.

I am convinced this is why so many entrepreneurs gravitate toward time hacking—a sadistic game of one-upping yourself with ever-increasing ridiculous time management tactics.

Without good delegation methods, you will also be that entrepreneur—splitting your day into fifteen-minute increments, taking meetings on the toilet, or learning how to make your hands type separate emails at the same time. It is madness! (Insert Kevin O' Leary's voice). You do not need a time hack to stay productive, you need a time-battered and tested approach to get the most from other people's time instead of your own.

I admit that there will be times when you need to be a tie-breaker on decisions, but this should be a luxury. Leave impromptu decisions for unforeseen emergencies.

UNPACKING THE TWO METHODS OF DELEGATION

Employees thrive when they can work within the two methods of process and principle. They thrive because the methods are so easy to learn. Let's look at an overview of both.

Principles and processes go together like peanut butter and jelly. Principle-driven delegation recognizes that personal empowerment is a safeguard for success. People feel free to make educated decisions when they have principles by which to govern their work life. Principle-driven delegation is like a set of guardrails in a bowling alley—you cannot help but head in the right direction. Like the name, this methodology helps employees navigate the unknown by giving them a principled (values-based) approach to drive their management of everyday decisions. Ones for which an old-fashioned plan cannot accomplish.

Principled delegation is powerful, but it is important to note that principles cannot speak to the granularity of task management—it just gets you headed in the right direction. Herein lies the need for a complementary process-driven approach.

Process-driven delegation is like the handlebars on a bike. It gives people the close-to-hand control they need to turn at a moment's notice as they pivot through the daily work in front of them. This form of delegation recognizes people need specific tools and techniques to execute their work effectively—so it gives them these controls. Best of all, processes keep people from overthinking their decisions. Processes keep them committed to simply getting their work done. Many watercooler debates about how the work *could* be done are solved by simply having good processes in place.

PRINCIPLES BEFORE PROCESSES

The best companies and the best leaders combine both types of delegation to empower people. They combine them to ensure their business runs smoothly—even when the owner is not physically present for the countless number of daily decisions that need to be made. We will go into more detail on how to use each method, but first, it is important to note that principle-driven delegation, whenever possible, should be implemented first. Process-driven delegation should fall within the boundaries of principle-driven delegation.

We lead with principles because they empower the employee—they know that if they do principled work, they exemplify your business culture and the specific things that make your brand unique. Good principles overcome a multitude of process sins. However, principles do not tell you about the specific way in which the work should be done, operationally. This is where processes come into play. Let's look at both in more detail.

PRINCIPLE-DRIVEN DELEGATION

A while back, I purchased a vehicle for my wife. The decision to buy was the result of months' worth of researching things like gas mileage, the vehicle's interior, and the best brand for our family. When we finally found the right vehicle, it made the purchasing decision easy. We took the vehicle home and were happy to have a new set of wheels, but we ran into a problem. We never received the tags for the vehicle. After calling the dealership, we discovered that the registration paperwork had been lost. It was a nightmare. But one of the dealership's associates hopped right on the issue. To show they cared about the urgency of the situation, they offered me two options; they would either drive 45 minutes to my office to get new paperwork signed, or fill my gas tank at the dealership if I came to fix the issue myself. This is an example of principle-driven delegation.

The associate could have reacted in fear, lied, or escalated the situation to their management, asking them what to do. But the dealership had a principle, do not make the customer pay for business mistakes, and if there is a mistake, make sure there is no out-of-pocket cost to solve the problem. The free gas also made the principle an extension of their brand.

Imagine the scenario if the associate had no operating principles available for which to solve the problem. If they were savvy, they might think to offer me a free tank of gas, but what if gas prices were high and it cost the business too much money that month? Or what if they had to get the problem solved by the salesperson who sold the vehicle? There would have to be a meeting to articulate the problem, the solution would have to be approved by one or more parties. They might even defer to negotiating with me, the customer, to see how upset I am before deciding on what to do next, finally following up with their manager on the next course of action. This would be a huge waste of time and I would be even more upset about their lack of initiative. My being upset might upset the associate, which would then upset the manager, and we would all just be playing a game of emotional Twister.

Without operating principles, employees default to working just to make you, the manager, happy. They will try and discern what you would do, or what will make you the least upset, and use that as a guide to get things done. But this approach is largely motivated by fear, of the unknown, associated with bad outcomes.

Not only that, doing what you would do might not always be the best decision. After all, you hired them for their skills too. This is the value in building out operating principles. When employees can rely on principles, they make decisions that are best for the customer or the team. They use these principles to highlight your brand and unique way of operating in the marketplace.

We see this play out in large corporations too. Nordstrom, the high-end clothing retailer, has been known to refund many things a customer returns up to five years from purchase, so long as the item can be found somewhere in its system (PopSugar, 2017). They operate on the principle of fairness. "We will do our best to take care of customers and deal with them fairly; we ask that our customers treat us fairly as well." states their site's return policy (Nordstrom, Returns & Exchanges, n.d.).

You might think this principle opens up opportunities for fraud or theft, but that risk is moot compared to the opportunity it gives employees to show gracious and accommodating customer service. Plus, this principle doubles as a sales strategy.

During an employee's onboarding process, they are taught to turn every return into a sale. The "rule of returns" actually doubles as lead generation. This principle of gracious returns empowers an employee to make decisions without approval from a manager, which makes them look good and makes the process of generating sales and serving customers distinctly unique in the world of retail (San Diego Reader, 2013).

An open return policy may not seem like any kind of management strategy, but it supports store managers in many ways. Consider the price and quality of the types of goods Nordstrom sells. Many items are pricey and take time to move off the rack. If an employee had to evaluate each return in a traditional fashion, they might easily get bogged down in the details of item quality, receipt accuracy, or even customer honesty. Not to mention, the need for managerial approval which is typical of larger purchases.

Imagine if the sales manager was required to evaluate every return above a certain price point. Not only would their time be drained significantly, but it could also make a loyal customer feel as though they were being interrogated. The outcome might lead to a diminished lifetime value of the customer and likely siphon the time of the sales manager as well.

By employing a principle-driven approach, instead of a typical returns process, the manager can get more done in-store with less time spent on nonessential details. Best of all it applies to multiple types of scenarios—and surely, at times, it results in additional sales and word-of-mouth marketing.

Principle-driven delegation is a derivative of a company's brand and values. Consider Nordstrom's mission statement, for example, a portion of it reads, "We work hard to make decisions in the best interest of our customers and those serving them." Nordstrom makes decisions based on the best interests of the customer and not the best interest of Nordstrom. This is a paradox because by simply serving customers, the customer serves them back. This would not happen, of course, but for the fact that they implemented this mission practically through their unique refund principle.

HOW TO CREATE MANAGERIAL PRINCIPLES

Principles manage decisions for you. The best principles tie back to your company's mission and values. When principles are tied to your brand, managerial decisions not only free up your time but also distinguish your business in the marketplace. Best of all, they empower your employees.

Here is how you create a delegatory principle. First, identify a task for which you do not want to manage edge cases or daily decisions. Second, abstract that decision and use it to create a guide for navigating the unknown.

For example, let's say you hired a chef for a hamburger joint. One of the chef's tasks is to buy ground beef each week from the local butcher shop. One week, the local butcher shop runs out of beef, and they have nothing to sell your chef. Without a principle, the chef will call you up, explain they have an emergency, and anxiously expound that customers will not be getting their hamburgers this week. This is a real pickle. Some might even call it a slider. To solve the problem, you call up the butcher, upset, because you have an agreement that states they promise to set aside x number of pounds of beef per week. You then panic, consider creating a custom menu, or worse, go full vegan for the next few days. You waste stress, energy, and time on the phone (the real crime). But with a principle in place, the chef knows that if one butcher is out of beef, then he is to contact other well-stocked butcher shops, so long as the beef is up to standard. In this scenario, the phone call never happens, the business continues to sell burgers, and you are none the wiser.

Without a managerial principle, the task is too hard-lined—buy two-hundred pounds of beef from Jerry's Beef Shop every Monday. And if Jerry gives them any problems, they call you and you call Jerry and sort it out Godfather style. With a principle, the task is broader—purchase ground beef on Monday mornings. The principle is that we only purchase and use Grade A beef in hamburgers. The process, (which we will get to shortly), is whenever possible, to buy from Jerry's Beef Shop with a maximum weekly budget of $1,500. With the principle in hand, the chef is empowered to find a different source for the beef without ever having to come to you, the self-proclaimed Manager of Meat, when a shortage arises. With this principle, the business continues to have a distinction from competitors with premium beef burgers, and the managerial implication of sourcing is never your concern.

As an entrepreneurial manager, you do need to be aware of deviations from the norm. If you have a partnership agreement with Jerry, and that agreement is consistently falling through, then it is your concern. But you only solve it when it becomes a consistent issue. You learn about these potential issues in your weekly meetings with your chef.

Finally, use problematic scenarios as an opportunity to move farther away from the work and strengthen the foundation of your managerial process. Little problems like the one in our example come up all the time. They provide an excellent opportunity to continue to build out new principles that empower your team, free up your time, and differentiate your business. They also go a long way in framing their accompanying processes.

PROCESS-DRIVEN DELEGATION

When I was seventeen, I drove a forklift through the wall of a machine shop. The building was not beyond repair, and no one was harmed—with the exception of my ego. I was what professional drivers call "forklift eager," but I was not forklift certified. If I had been certified, or at the very least trained, then I likely would not have driven the forklift through the unsuspecting wall, and I would have moved on to the big kahuna—the industrial-sized forklift. This would have been a promotion, and then I would have been able to delegate out all the wall-ruining to someone else. At least, that is what I like to tell myself.

At the time, the business I worked for had a startup mantra to move fast and break stuff. No problem there, but I would have benefited from some practical, on-the-job training so I could do my work effectively. What both the company and the forklift suffered from was a lack of managerial process.

The company was not so different from other businesses in the throes of hiring, in that, they had to move quickly and needed able bodies to do so. But without processes to inform how an employee was to operate within their role, everything within the role was open to interpretation. Sadly, busy managers, even the ones who really care about good delivery, can suffer from a "they'll figure it out" mindset. I say suffer because the employee is the one who has to struggle through the lack of process and figure things out for themselves. This struggle leads to a breakdown in efficiency.

PROCESSES IN A BUSINESS

There are many types of processes within a business, so we are only going to focus on processes that help an employee do their job. To this end, we will look at how to build task-oriented processes, meaning tasks that can be repeated over and over again.

Repeatability within a role, especially with entrepreneurship, can feel like a death sentence. Repeatable work can feel like that familiar Wile E. Coyote cartoon where you are clocking in every day, only to get beaten by dogged tasks repeatedly. However, without the benefit of repeatable work, your business will be driven by employee personality, customer urgency, and the endless (even unimaginable) ways every individual prefers to work.

When a business is very small, these oddities do not feel like a problem. In fact, many entrepreneurs face the temptation to let someone with talent figure out the details. The only problem here is that the process will change when they change, when they move on to another job, or if they happen to do something unexpected. This is especially true when a company begins to grow larger, and you have multiple employees doing the same type of work.

A large company I consulted with had teams of people who worked on cataloging products and sorting their respective financial details. They did this work for well over two decades, however, every person had a different approach. This led to an error rate of over 80 percent, which in turn, led to hundreds of thousands of dollars in lost time, research, and data correction. The result was that smaller businesses could compete with them regardless of their large retail footprint. Had they diverted their energy into building processes, instead of simply shoveling as much product categorization work as possible, they would have gotten more done with fewer errors and fewer people.

This is the paradox of process. When a business is growing and things feel urgent, the outcome of the work seems like the most urgent thing to pursue. However, if you simply pursue getting the work done, the business will grow, but it will grow unwieldy. It will become so unwieldy that the amount of incoming business actually cripples the business itself. This leads to layoffs, lost clients, and a lack of positive brand perception in the market.

However, if you can build supportive processes now, your employees will get more done and you can rest assured that your business will be able to scale effectively. Not only will you benefit from building a scalable business, but the established ways of working will not disappear with the inevitable turnover that happens in a business.

TASK-CENTERED PROCESSES

So how do you build really good, task-centered processes? Just like a good meatball sub, task-centered processes have three parts: Go-No-Go's, task outcomes, and task steps.

TASK GO-NO-GO

During the Apollo missions, NASA used a status checklist, called a Go-No-Go, which included about fifteen different areas of focus, ranging from things like booster integrity, guidance monitoring, and general procedures. All of these areas of focus had to be accounted for before the rocket could launch. From the outside, it might appear that the space flight was as simple as pressing a button, launching the rocket, and going to the moon. But there were a host of initial details that had to be in play before the launch began. If something did not pass a checkpoint, the next task could not begin. These types of details compose a G/NG.

How often have you started a project or gotten deep into the work, only to realize you missed something before you began? Once you realize the mistake, you might circle back to fix it, compensate for the next time it occurs, or blame your notes app for not reminding you of the things you were supposed to set up first. If it is just you that missed something, it is only your time wasted. The fire is controlled. But without a clear Go-No-Go for your employees, your team will suffer from a lack of effective execution. We will use this example to create Task Go-No-Go's in your business.

First thing to remember is that a Task Go-No-Go is not simply a kick-off meeting or checkpoint. A TG/NG is a set of criteria that must be met before the work can begin. You use TG/NGs to ensure your employee has done their due diligence before they begin a particular type of work. Consider it a type of simplified, pre-flight checklist.

The question for your business, and specifically the unique work you will delegate to employees, is what steps do employees need to take first to ensure a task will be successful before they start the work? The answer is a checklist, either mental or physical, that tells an employee they can start a task.

The list itself can be very short, even one item, but the point is to create a definitive marker—a TG/NG moment before the work starts—so you know the subsequent task will be executed with the highest possibility of success. A few examples of TG/NGs in different businesses are: a construction project getting proper permits before beginning work, a web development agency setting up a development environment before the work of coding, a bed-and-breakfast putting a mint on the pillow before showing a guest to the room, and a tanning salon cleaning the room before renting it out.

Of course, with all these examples, you could argue for a different first step, or even that the step is not necessary at all. And that is partially the point, your business is defined by its brand, its value proposition, and the way in which the work is done. You could skip the mint on the pillow, but you missed the opportunity to delight the customer. You could skip cleaning the tanning salon room but might eventually deal with the odor. You could skip getting the right permits, but you risk getting shut down by the city. You could skip setting up a web development environment before a project as well, but then you risk your code to the security of someone's local machine.

The Task Go-No-Go is great for book-ending a set of tasks together too. If you need to delegate work that includes large, multi-day, or highly detailed work, then you can use this as a way to check and see if a task is really finished and the next is ready to begin.

Outcomes are good, and steps are enlightening, but TG/NGs make sure you are ready to begin the work. Use them to build excellent execution processes and to guide your employees in high-quality, repeatable work. A good TG/NG positions the work for a good outcome.

TASK OUTCOMES

Good throughput of work begins with the outcome in mind. A task outcome is what the result of a particular task is meant to achieve. Sometimes this is called a deliverable, other times this is called something looser like a "definition of completion,"

For example, if the task in question is making a hamburger, the outcome of making a hamburger is a hamburger sandwich, packaged and plated. If the task is a monthly profit and loss statement, then the outcome is a fully balanced finance sheet. If the task is changing the oil in a car, the outcome is a parked and vacuumed car, which has been adequately serviced with oil.

Notice the specificity in the last example. The specificity is what makes for a good outcome. If you were to give the task of changing the oil to three different but highly experienced mechanics, there is a good chance they may all have a different definition of what an oil change might include. One mechanic may simply change the oil and consider the job complete. Another mechanic may ask what type of oil the owner desires and then proceed to change the oil. Yet another mechanic may simply check to see if the oil needs to be replaced, and if they think it still has some mileage, return the vehicle and call it a day. In our example, the task of changing oil was paired with vacuuming out the car and parking it in front of the shop.

So here is the point, if you do not define the outcome, the outcome will be defined by the personality and experience of the person doing the work. So, you need to define the outcome of a task before you can delegate the task. Once you have defined the outcome, you can define the steps toward that outcome.

TASK STEPS

An outcome is the output of a set of steps that lead up to task completion. You get to one by reverse-engineering what you want to see. To the extent possible, you optimize the steps for profitability, efficiency, and customer delight.

For example, if you were to assign the task of creating a single page for a website to someone, the steps might include an initial client meeting, creating a rough mockup, authoring the copywriting, designing a high-fidelity prototype, testing the prototype, and then delivering the prototype to a website engineer for coding. There are six steps before the task is considered complete. Without these steps, someone might just assume they could create the prototype and then have a client meeting or skip to the end and simply have it developed based on the design of other pages on the site. There is a whole mix of possibilities in between.

The steps exist so that expectations can be set, time can be managed, and profit can be predicted in a meaningful way. Steps for tasks should be comprised of meaningful chunks of work that have clear lines of delineation.

In your business, spend some time considering where the lines of delineation fall between tasks. You will find new opportunities to create efficiency and customer delight. Now let's look at how to build a task template.

HOW TO BUILD A PROCESS-DRIVEN TASK TEMPLATE

A process-driven task consists of the Task Go-No-Go, the Task Steps, and the Task Outcome. While it is best to create a task template before you delegate, you can also choose to reverse engineer a task and break it down into a template as well. In fact, you can use the following process to easily identify new tasks and templatize them as the business and the work changes and grows. Let's look at a quick example, and then you can create your own.

Task Type: Landscape a small business.

Task Go-No-Go: Make sure sprinklers are turned off. Pick up all trash and litter. Inform the tenant of mowing duration.

Task Steps: Mow lawn. Edge boundaries, sidewalks, fence. Rake up trimmings

Task Go-No-Go: Walk through finished work with tenant. Tenant sign-offs on work.

Task Outcome: The campus is fully landscaped and manicured.

Download The Free Template!

Get the **Task Go/No Go** template along with other great tools included with this book at:

https://piercebrantley.co/NYJ-downloads

Process-driven tasks are the simplest way to create repeatable chunks of work within your organization. When you template tasks, you make work easy to hand off and easy to modify in the future. Best of all, you have a turnkey approach that will benefit new employees as well.

When you combine process-driven delegation with principle-driven delegation, you wield a powerful managerial ability. Combined, they will enable you to be more trusting of the work being done when you are not around to scc it happen. If you continue to combine both principles and processes at a high standard, you create something new—a good company culture.

CHAPTER 14

HOW TO MANAGE FOR LONG-TERM SUCCESS

IF YOU WANT TO GO FAST, GO BY YOURSELF. If you want to go far, go together. This ancient proverb does not just apply to Mario Kart. To sustain success in your business, your team must be willing to go the distance with you. You see, The Elevator Effect is powerful, but it has its limits.

The reason is simple, managerial expectations guide but they do not always inspire. Empowerment, however, which is the act of distributing power, will let someone guide themselves.

Empowerment returns power to the people. Empowerment adds weight to delegation. When an employee values their work, they will carry the work further; this, in turn, keeps your time returned to you and continues to foster organic innovation in your company.

Imagine an employee staying with you for years, not months or seasons. Imagine not needing to retrain, rehire, or pivot for a role simply because an employee chose to make a career change. Long-term retention like this is possible, but it requires two key commitments from you. First, you must invest in the individual's success. Second, you must inspire them to invest in the vision of your business.

These two commitments, from you, will confirm to your employee that their time is invested in the right type of work. Without this commitment from you, the work is simply an exchange of value. Their time for your money. The exchange is a tactical need, not an intrinsic benefit.

Until now, we simply used The Elevator Effect to recover your time. This leverage, however, is not sustainable through managerial skills alone. Skill can tune an instrument, but the soul alone can make it play. If you want the effects of delegation to be sustainable, you will need to employ what I like to call Tactical Leadership. Tactical Leadership keeps the soul of your business alive.

TACTICAL LEADERSHIP

An architect I know was asked to give a big presentation for their executive team. The request was made by the manager and the entire team was involved in the preparation. The team prepared every detail for their manager, but for one of the employees, the time of the presentation was very early—about 12:30 in the morning. Even though their time zone was much different from the one in which the presentation was to be given, they still wanted to do well with their boss and to represent their hard work.

The day before the presentation, the architect let the employee know they were off the hook if they did not want to join the call— the meeting was very late, after all. But the late-night lead persisted, voicing how much the project meant to them.

On the day of the presentation, the time zoned employee spoke first. They had barely begun when the architect received a call from the manager who set up the meeting. "Get them off the presentation immediately! Who thought it was a good idea to let them speak? I never said they could speak. Was this your idea?" they demanded. "They want to represent their work," the architect responded. "If they want representation then they need to go to another company. This is not a team, this is a presentation, and they are ruining it. Take over for them now!" the manager insisted. The architect got off the call, interrupted the employee speaking, and took over their remaining slides to appease the manager.

Afterward, the architect explained to the employee that the manager had not wanted them to speak and apologized for butting in on their presentation. But the damage was permanent. The manager, however, got what they wanted. The presentation was a success, the project was funded, and everyone who made decisions went home happy. From the outside, the manager did his job.

MANAGER, LEADER, OR BOTH?

Since the dawn of the managerial man, pundits have debated whether managers can be leaders or leaders, managers. The sentiment seems to be that the two roles are a bit like cats and dogs. Some people prefer one, others the latter. Occasionally they can live in the same house, but it is rare and the people who allow it are weird.

Part of the problem in this debate is the idea that leaders and managers are divided into long-term thinkers and short-term thinkers. Leaders inspire people to pursue the future. Managers hold people's feet to the fiery present reality. Together, they inspire a bright and burning future for the employee.

The thinking goes that an organization needs both mindsets. This is true. Both types of thinking help a team produce good results for a business, but this does not mean the two roles are mutually exclusive. A person can inspire action and define the right steps as well—sometimes in the same breath.

Employees need inspiration and instruction. Together, they help an employee stay vested in a company. Employees need these things from you. But this does not mean you need to go get a certification as a Maxwell Coach to start delegating work. Although if you do, I am sure you will not be disappointed.

You do not need to be a renowned leader to motivate people. You are not going for Oprah status. However, if you do want to motivate your team members, you will benefit from using some Tactical Leadership.

FOR ENTREPRENEURS

Tactical Leadership is leadership for people who need to motivate people to do their work, do it well, and feel connected to the vision of the company. Tactical leadership is meant for the manager. It is not meant for the person who wants to draw in crowds of thousands and one-up Tony Robbins at his next conference in Florida. Tactical leadership focuses on what continually keeps a person motivated to work for a company so that the effects of delegation persist through all the unexpected days that come with work life. Tactical leadership allows you to continue leveraging the benefits of The Elevator Effect without needing to be a figurehead—at least all the time.

Earlier we said an individual needs two things to say connected to their work. Those two things were your investment in the individual's success and their vested interest in the business's vision. When you combine these two practical elements of leadership together, you can sustain your hard work and effectively delegate work to other people from a visionary perspective. This is where empowerment begins.

INVESTING IN THE INDIVIDUAL

In game theory, there are two types of motivation. There is intrinsic motivation, which is the type of motivation that is built into us. Then there is extrinsic motivation, which is the type of motivation that keeps us motivated because of some kind of external reward. Good games blend both types of motivation to keep a player motivated throughout the ups and downs of gameplay. The result, in a good game, is play that feels as though it mirrors real life, which makes the experience all the more interesting and exciting. To the player, the progress in the game feels real because, as far as the brain is concerned, it is.

Good managers are good motivators. Good managers know how to build varying types of motivations into the work environment—keeping a worker interested and excited about what they do. Good motivators also know that people are motivated by different rewards and different factors, both internal and external. Some employees care a lot about their title but not as much about pay scale. Others only care about pay scale and couldn't care less about what their job description is at work. These are just two examples. The differences in preference are endless, so it is in your best interest to try and ascertain what keeps each individual employee engaged in their respective role.

THREE FUNDAMENTALS TO INVESTING IN PEOPLE

There are three simple ways to motivate a person. Each one supports The Elevator Effect in its own special way. The first is to know how an employee thinks and solves problems, the second is to celebrate their successes, and the third is to support their career. Leaders who practice these three fundamentals find they worry less about the quality of work getting done. They worry less because the employee feels meaningfully connected to their work and the business. When you combine these three fundamentals, you also create a culture that champions the people who take their work seriously. This culture begins to work for you as well, perpetuating the behavior you want to see from future managers you may promote or hire.

THEIR PERSONALITY

People are motivated to work for you when you can demonstrate you appreciate the way they approach their work. People perceive their approach to work uniquely. They can also take their approach very personally, so it benefits you to understand the way they think as opposed to you or another team member.

Take, for example, my coffee-drinking colleague. A colleague I knew never cleaned out the office coffee machine after making a cup of coffee. Whenever someone else in the office wanted a cup of coffee, they would have to remove the person's disposable coffee container and even get new water for the machine. This felt like pure, uncaffeinated laziness on the part of the offending colleague. That is until they volunteered some personal trivia one afternoon.

Our coffee culprit took cleanliness and beverage taste very seriously. They supposed the water in the coffee maker might actually take on the taste of their drink if someone chose a different flavored beverage than them. So as an act of kindness, they left their trash in the coffee machine. The reasoning was that someone may want to make an educated decision about whether to clean the entire machine before making a cup of Columbian robusta—just as they themselves would do. The colleague perceived their behavior as thoughtful.

There are endless differences in the way people work and behave on the job. One of the ways you can discover this work perception is with a personality test. A personality test, while not exhaustive, will give you insight into the way people think and feel about their role.

A BLUE CHIP PERSONALITY

One of my favorite stories about how companies use personality tests was at General Electric. While I attended a virtual leadership summit, Jeff Immelt, GE's CEO and successor to Jack Welsh at the time, shared how they built worker profiles based on the work of their highest performers. They used these special profiles to predict and evaluate a person's potential for promotion within the organization. The thinking was simple, if someone was especially talented and attuned to a certain type of work, they would have a higher likelihood of success in the role. The profile, built on successful working habits, seemed to prove it.

You do not need the sophistication of GE to build a high-caliber team. But if you know the personality types of the people who work for you, it will help a great deal. If you know how someone thinks about themselves and how they interpret their work, you will blow past all kinds of misunderstandings when work gets tough.

AVAILABILITY OF TESTS

There are several personality tests available to you now and many volumes on the subject, so I will not try and persuade you on any one particular framework here. But some of my favorites are the Myers Briggs, Enneagram, and StrengthsFinder 2.0 from Gallup. In an executive role, I have also taken DiSC from Wiley. I found it to be an enlightening tool. I am a High D if you are curious.

The purpose of using a personality test is to help you and the employee gain a little self-awareness about how the employee approaches their work. The test does not need to be exhaustive or scientific either. People are nuanced. You just want to get acquainted with their general behavior.

I recommend you give a new hire a personality test during onboarding or perhaps in one of their reporting meetings. After they take the test, ask them to talk through their results and how they feel about what the test has revealed. Pay attention to where they get excited and deeply connect with a result. If you really want to be astute, pay even closer attention to where they feel the test got them wrong.

When the employee comes across results they feel misrepresent their personality, ask them why. You will often discover important information about how they see themselves. The discussion will foster comradery too. I saw this firsthand with an employee in a creative role.

One day, while managing a digital product team, an employee came to me about a frustration they had with a colleague on a different team. The offending colleague in question was reportedly dismissing other people's work. To make matters worse, they were also giving new instructions to people about how to do their jobs. Folks were frustrated, and at face value, the behavior seemed disrespectful to the team. Not to mention, their advice made my team less productive.

However, after a little digging, it was clear the individual was actually very good at problem-solving and able to see workloads from multiple angles. Because of my familiarity with personality types, I guessed their profile based on their behavior. From there, I asked my team member to change the way they responded to the person based on this new understanding. They took my advice and changed their approach the next time they met.

The change in communication worked like a charm. From then on, my team member was able to navigate the person's strong personality type.

Now, I could have assumed the afflicting employee had overstepped their bounds. Their actions could have resulted in a pink slip and a rehire. While this decision would have solved the immediate offense, it also would have restarted the delegatory process.

With just a little effort and time, you can build a sort of sixth sense about how people like to work—even when you do not know them very well. This intuition will be seen by others. Soon, you will be perceived as a leader, which will further aid your ability to delegate effectively. Once you understand the way people think, you can celebrate their successes even more.

CELEBRATING SUCCESS

When you know how someone thinks, you can celebrate the special ways in which they achieve results for your company. And when you celebrate the achievements of others, you are also less likely to draw attention back to yourself.

As entrepreneurial managers, we celebrate the successes of others, in part, because they deserve to be celebrated. But we also celebrate their successes so we do not fall into the trap of *trying* to act managerial.

HARD-LINED APPROACH

I have seen a bizarre pattern with new managers wherein they think they need to *act* managerial in order to motivate people effectively. The behavior is like fake-it-till-you-make-it but worse because cubicles are involved.

This hard-lined approach could not be less effective. People work for a company for a variety of external reasons, the least of which, at first, is the manager. The obvious reason being that they have not worked with them long enough to know if the relationship is a good fit. What motivates someone to take a job has very little to do with the person they work for, even if they liked the manager during the interview process. The reason this is important is that if the manager did not play a role in motivating the person to take the job, there is very little the manager can do to keep them there if the person gets the sense they are not valued by their manager.

TWO MANAGERS, ONE MISTAKE

In my early twenties, I took an internship as a digital marketing associate. My team and I got along well, and we enjoyed the work. Other teams, however, had very high turnover. Key leaders were leaving regularly and at first, it was hard to tell why—until a corporate training meeting we had with one of the leaders in upper management. During the meeting, the individual instructed us on what they saw as praiseworthy and promotable work. As they said, next to nothing was worthy of promotion unless you earned their respect.

In the meeting, they laid out a dismal vision for what was promotable worthy behavior. If you showed up every day and did your job, you would get no recognition. This was the job you were hired to do, and you should not get praised for doing the bare minimum, they reasoned. The second tier was coming early and staying late. Overcommitment was commitment. If you extended your time commitment, it showed the manager you cared. But they wanted to see you do this regularly so that they knew you were really vested in the organization's success. The third tier was doing work above and beyond your role. In this capacity, you would take initiative, as they called it, and do things for which you were not hired to do. If you did extra work, along with all the other things, then you would be worthy of respect and recognition. Many of their people went on to be recognized at other jobs. This manager was a pioneer of the quiet quitting phenomenon we are seeing today.

A second manager I knew had a similar mantra but in the context of positive feedback (corporate decoder ring for 'encouragement'). In one notable case, they intentionally cut a salesperson out of a client meeting because they personally did not feel respected by the salesperson—even though the salesperson had closed a lot of deals for the company. When they were asked why they cut the salesperson out of the meeting they said, "On principle, I do not encourage people. If someone gets the sense they are performing well, then I have no way to keep them in line when I want something done." They left the salesperson out of the meeting in hopes that it would motivate them to work harder for their respect. This salesperson too, went on to find other work.

As entrepreneurial managers, it can sometimes feel overly gracious to recognize and praise behavior that someone is paid to do. After all, we work with little to no encouragement for our efforts. But the truth is that the employee does not have to work for our company if they do not want to. Gratitude from the managing entrepreneur is a good and necessary character trait. Doing so will keep people motivated in their roles.

Managerial gratitude extends to times when an employee makes a mistake as well. The old adage, "praise in public and correct in private," is a golden rule for anyone who wants to delegate effectively. A job is not the military, and a manager is not a drill instructor. Of course, this does not mean you cannot be firm or direct. Straightforward communication is always helpful. Just remember to celebrate the person doing the work whenever you get the chance.

A manager I had while in an engineering role modeled this gracious behavior very well. During my first few weeks on the job, I crashed the startup's e-commerce website—the main source of income for the company. When my manager came up to my desk, I was in a panic. "I am sorry I crashed your website," I said in a sweat.

"It is *our* site," they responded. "I know you will fix it." In two breaths they communicated the co-ownership of work and the trust they had in my role. Their gracious response calmed my nerves, and I was able to fix the problem shortly after. If they had come into my office upset, or in a panic themselves, I likely would have perpetuated the problem as my energy would have been spent trying to make them happy.

After the site was up and running again, we had a meeting to go over the reason the problem surfaced and how to avoid it in the future. It turns out the code I inherited was badly written in the first place and contributed to the problem. My manager thanked me for diligently fixing the issue and that crash never came up again.

When we celebrate our employees, it shows we are vested in their success. It also demonstrates that we recognize that they could spend their time with any company and that we respect their decision in choosing our own. Best of all, celebrating successes actively puts away the Antivalues we discussed earlier, making us more trusting and emotionally intelligent leaders.

INVESTING IN THEIR CAREER

Earlier we discovered that trust, and not tasks, is what we truly delegate to another person. Trust is proportional. You give trust in proportion to your comfort with risk as well as an individual's competency. One practical way to continue to grow your trust in a person, as well as their own competency on the job, is to intentionally invest in their career. You do this through some form of continued education.

While you can invest in a person's career at any point, your best bet is to start when you both are on the fourth floor, *Show What You Do*. If you are deepening their role or giving them oversight over new responsibilities, demonstrate your commitment to their success by investing in their success.

Now, this does not mean that you need to go out and fund an MBA for the person, but I certainly know many companies that do provide this type of benefit. Yes, education can be expensive, but it is not nearly as expensive as starting from scratch in the hiring process or losing the experience of the individual. Not to mention, their new learnings will be leveraged by your business and the education is normally some type of write-off. I am no accountant, of course, you should have your tax team advise if this would be the case for you. At the very least, however, provide some access to leadership training, industry conferences, or certifications that support the growth of the individual.

I have heard managers lament over how much money they lose when employees go to conferences. But I think, personally, this is the wrong perspective. Good decisions have a monetary value to them. Just ask any business consultant worth their title. If your employees are more capable than your competition, then their decision-making skills are more effective as well. Moreover, they are likely to stay with a company longer too.

Take, for example, Fiat Chrysler Automobiles. FCA partnered with Strayer University to offer dealership employees the opportunity to earn a degree for free. According to 2017 data, those dealerships experienced a retention rate of nearly 40 percent. Better still, the dealerships that participated saw revenue grow 17 percent, compared to nonparticipating dealers (Why Companies Should Pay for Employees to Further Their Education, *Harvard Business Review*, October 19, 2020).

TIP FOR CONTINUED EDUCATION

If you do choose to invest in an employee's education, a helpful strategy is to amend an employee's contract. The thought is, if they do get some continued education benefit through the business, they must commit themselves for an additional amount of time. If they leave early, they repay the money invested in them. But normally, you will not need this to be enforced.

I have invested in the education of my team members, and they stayed with the company long after I left, simply because they knew the company was invested in their success. Overall, continued education is a win-win for the individual and the business, regardless of the cost.

When you know how a person thinks, you celebrate how their thinking leads to success, and when you invest in their continued success, your guidance as a manager will go all the further. This is because people will now know both what's expected of them and that those expectations are supported by your goodwill. You will also worry less about their work because people will feel meaningfully connected to their jobs. Best of all, you plant the seeds of culture-building, which keep the work working for you.

COMMITTING TO THE VISION

Joel A. Barker, the futurist and pioneer of paradigm shifts once said, "Vision without action is merely a dream. Action without vision just passes the time. Vision with action can change the world." He nailed it. When entrepreneurs begin their managerial journey, their primary concern is with recovering their time. Once their time has been recovered, their primary concern is with how other people spend their time.

If the way people spend their time is simply connected to a task, to mindless and obedient action, then almost anything can persuade them to leave their jobs. However, if they understand the vision of the organization and how their work is changing their world, no matter how small that world may be, then their work has meaning.

FINAL THOUGHTS ON VISION

These three fundamentals cement an employee's feeling of connection to their work and your business. If you implement them, the employee will know you support them. The only remaining question is whether they feel as if they are connected to the future of your business. This sense of connection is what we call vision. Vision is the compass. Vision tells the employee where they are headed. Vision tells the employee their work serves more than just themselves or your wishes. Vision is necessary for their continual investment in their jobs and the business.

One of the tech businesses I helped lead did this very well. Once a month, leadership would gather all the employees together, and re-iterate the vision of the business. This included how the business advanced toward goals and how the team supported the advancement.

In this meeting, leadership could have simply called out recent successes. But they went a step further and produced special videos that celebrated the people who created the successes too. In these special videos, a person would be highlighted for their recent achievements, but the video also showcased interviews of people who communicated why they valued the person in the spotlight. By the end of the video, the highlighted person would be smiling ear-to-ear, maybe even crying just a bit as they saw how much they meant to their team.

You do not need a media team to create highlight reels of your employees just to show them appreciation. But you can still create a celebratory culture by publicly praising good work. A lot of work does not feel particularly visionary while it is being accomplished. Digging trenches is rarely fun, but if trenches help win the war, and winning the war protects a nation, then trench-digging is visionary. Remind people of how their work is part of the greater good your business is doing in the world. People will continue to do good work if you do.

You will have success when you invest in the success of your people. You invest in the success of your people by knowing who they are, how they think, and connecting them with the vision of your business. When you have a business full of vision-linked workers, you can out-leverage your competition and your business challenges. You can trust people to get the work done even when you are not there to see it accomplished. Best of all, you can happily say, "that is not my job!"

HIRE PIERCE TO SPEAK AT YOUR NEXT EVENT

Brantley is a dynamic speaker—he uses the emotion of story, the power of data, and the influence of a master communicator to bring your audience into new revelations about how to live and run their businesses.

Some topics Brantley speaks on:

Innovation

Management

Entrepreneurship

Technology & Business

Faith & Business (Kingdom Entrepreneurship)

Visit https://piercebrantley.co/speaking/ to learn more about scheduling him for your next event.

SOURCES

On Burnout

https://hbr.org/2018/04/what-makes-entrepreneurs-burn-out

Planning Fallacy

https://en.wikipedia.org/wiki/Planning_fallacy

Assemble a Truck

https://www.motorbiscuit.com/how-long-does-it-take-to-assemble-a-pickup-truck/

Nordstrom

https://www.popsugar.com/fashion/Nordstrom-Secrets-Revealed-43419720

https://www.sandiegoreader.com/news/2013/mar/13/cover-selling-service-nordstrom/

https://www.nordstrom.com/browse/customer-service/return-policy

Company Culture

https://academiccommons.columbia.edu/doi/10.7916/D8DV1S08

https://hbr.org/sponsored/2020/10/why-companies-should-pay-for-employees-to-further-their-education

CPSIA information can be obtained
at www.ICGtesting.com
Printed in the USA
JSHW082328271122
33920JS00001B/5